Teaching Strategies of Success

C. Bernard Solomon, PhD

STUDIO
OF BOOKS
THE SPACE FOR YOUR MESSAGE

Studio of Books LLC
5900 Balcones Drive Suite 100
Austin, Texas 78731
www.studioofbooks.org
Hotline: (254) 800-1183

Ordering Information:
Special discounts are available on quantity purchases by corporations, associations, and others. For details, contact the publisher at the address above.

Printed in the United States of America.

ISBN-13: Softcover   978-1-964928-59-3
          eBook   978-1-964928-60-9
          Hardback

Table *of* Contents

Chapter 1

INTRODUCTION AND PURPOSE

Introduction

The ideas shared in this book are based on my experiences from multiple perspectives – educational researcher, rural public school educator, inner city public school educator, building level public school administrator, district level public school administrator and parent. By no means is this book designed to be an all-inclusive manual to follow.

It is important that you know more about me and my experiences to help you feel more comfortable accepting the suggestions offered in this book. Throughout the book, I will offer a mixture of research and personal experience to support many of the topics that are discussed. It is my experience that educators want to see research but they desire even more to know how the concept has worked during the implementation phase. Therefore, I have made it a priority to suggest the actions educators should take during the implementation phase to create a higher probability that the strategies offered will yield successful outcomes.

It is my hope that you find this book to be a resource filled with valuable strategies from the perspective of both an educational researcher and practitioner. Oftentimes books of this nature are written from one perspective or the other. The beauty of this book is you get both! However, the suggestions provided are based on a summation of my personal research and past experiences. Therefore, you should do your homework and review relevant educational literature and research studies to validate the concepts for yourself. I have offered a few resources at the end of the book to get you started. Although most of the ideas shared can be applied to most age groups, it is still up to you to make adaptations for your specific set of students.

As I mentioned earlier, I am sharing experiences from multiple perspectives. I served as a public school teacher in both rural and inner-city classrooms for six years. Both of these categories of schools had their own unique challenges that taught me some valuable experience. There were challenges that created obstacles and setbacks that I had to overcome. Some of the challenges and obstacles involved areas such as classroom resources, parental involvement, community engagement, and professional development opportunities.

Another perspective I bring is that of a researcher. I paused my teaching career to attend graduate school as a full-time student. This was after earning a master's degree in teaching and a graduate certificate of advanced studies in educational administration as I simultaneously fulfilled the duties of a classroom teacher. As a full-time researcher, I spent countless hours reviewing and conducting research studies on effective teaching and the factors that impact teacher success. I also assisted my doctoral program advisor, Dr. Jerry Valentine, with numerous school visits to help train teachers on ways to increase teacher effectiveness and student engagement using the Instructional Practices Inventory (IPI) that he developed. Based on research from the IPI, teachers and schools who used IPI strategies with fidelity experienced higher student achievement growth.

My perspective as a public school administrator helps to guide the selection of strategies shared in this book. The 13-year period I spent as a building principal included many professional development sessions on effective teaching resources and programs, and faculty problem solving discussions on teaching strategies. Throughout my tenure as a building administrator, I conducted thousands of classroom observations. I was able to witness exemplary teaching and provide constructive feedback when improvement was needed.

Additionally, I bring a public school district administrator perspective. I served as a human resources director of certificated and salaried personnel. In this role I was able to visit schools and interact with both educators and administrators. This helped me to see a wider range of teaching expectations and practices being implemented in classrooms throughout the district. This experience was a very significant part of increasing my knowledge base on effective teaching strategies.

The last perspective, but equally as important, is my perspective as a parent. As my own children attended school and encountered different teachers, I learned a tremendous amount about how to set the expectations for both my children and the teachers who taught them. I also gained more insight on the various teaching and communication styles students and parents must navigate as part of their school experience. My experience as a parent has helped me share with teachers the importance of incorporating strategies that will assist parents. You will see more on this in the chapter dedicated to school-home-community partnership.

The multiple perspectives I have mentioned serve as part of the foundation of this book. In addition to my perspectives, there is some evidence that the strategies offered in this book have been a major reason for many of the positive results throughout the years. I believe it is important to share some additional evidence that supports why I feel somewhat qualified to share my ideas with other educators.

During my years as a teacher and administrator, there were many accomplishments along the way that are worth noting. This is not an all-inclusive list but it does capture some major areas that most educators and school systems monitor. Listed below are some of the noteworthy accomplishments both working as a teacher and as an administrator working with teachers.

Teacher

- Improved class passing rate to over 95% in content courses taught.

- Consistently had over 95% homework completion.

- Improved classroom office referrals from over 30 for the year to less than five each year.

- Improved state test scores in math for at least 75% of the students taught each year.

- Improved parent engagement at conferences, events, and programs.

Administrator

- Teachers achieved five consecutive years of growth in science on the state assessment.

- Teachers decreased the achievement gap in math and science for African American, special education, and free or reduced lunch students on state assessment consistently each year.

- Consistently reduced out of school suspensions.

- Consistently increased parent engagement and community partnerships.

- Created a student-centered culture to prioritize the wellbeing of all students.

There are many more points to include, but I believe this gives you an idea of some of the positive results I've been fortunate to experience as a teacher and administrator. If I included all the accomplishments, that could be a book of its own. Hopefully, this is enough to get your attention so that you will at least consider what I am offering in this book.

The ideas in this book include a perspective generated from the thousands of interactions with teachers, students, parents, and community groups over more than 25 years. Along the way, there have been observations and conversations that have helped shape my views on teaching and learning. The ideas shared in this book are not solely from my efforts. Most of the situations I share involved the help and support of many others. Therefore, it should be noted that when you see "I" it can also mean "we" in many of the situations.

Both as a teacher and administrator, others did not always agree. However, after discussions and collaboration there inevitably was usually a better method or decision than the original one. I believe this ultimately yielded better results than would have originally been achieved. Therefore, it is important to note that I am not by any means claiming to be an expert who has operated alone without the collaboration and support of many other individuals and groups along the way. Please be sure to keep this in mind when reading the book.

Also, keep in mind that this is my perspective and research on the effectiveness of the strategies I share in this book. More than likely some of the teachers who taught with me or those I supervised might remember some of the details differently than I have explained them. It is unlikely any two people will share the exact same perspective. Of course, if they want their versions to be told, they can write their own book!

As I reflect on the experiences I gained during my life, I have vivid memories of the many complex situations that caused me to grapple with my own thoughts and emotions. I imagine you have had some similar experiences when working with complex situations involving students, parents and teacher colleagues. Through it all, I submit to you that once you have read this book you will realize that there are many more things to celebrate and cherish than things to fret about. It really will come down to the mindset you have and the degree to which you decide to take control of your destiny.

Hopefully, you will find a variety of strategies in this book to help provide you with the confidence and reassurance you need to be an effective educator. As the saying goes, *"It's not rocket science."* I hope to show you that teaching is not as difficult as many people think it is.

Purpose

This book is written to provide insight to teachers in a manner that should help ease some of the anxiety associated with educating students. The primary purpose is to provide teachers with some strategies that should yield positive outcomes for their students. There is an intentional focus on both school and home because these are the two locations that students spend most of their time. I suggest that if teachers use strategies that have a positive impact on their student's lives in these two environments, they will be highly successful.

The reality is there are many challenges facing teachers today. As teachers try to help students navigate through their educational journey, it is important to recognize the challenges but it is even more important to determine how to overcome those challenges. Along the way, there will be times when it seems as though you are fighting against the world.

For example, you may hear from a student about what other students are allowed to do in your classroom, what other teachers are allowing their students to do in their classroom, or what other schools are allowing their students to do. You may also hear students accuse you of favoritism. You might have a significant number of students who are behaviorally or academically challenged. Colleagues may work against you or gossip about you. Your administrator may not provide the support you feel is needed.

In addition to all of this, parents may give you push back or even become irate about a situation. You may be asked to take on more responsibilities than you have time to handle. The district office might be overwhelming teachers with too many initiatives or programs. The list could go on and on. Rather than continue depressing you with a longer list, I will narrow the list down to some major challenges that I believe are essential to discuss.

Throughout this book, I will dive deeper into six challenges that I believe are the most important for teachers to overcome. These six challenges are based on the many situations I have experienced as a teacher, administrator, and parent. These challenges can become major obstacles if not handled effectively. I will address these challenges in the subsequent chapters.

First, in Chapter 2, I address the challenge of understanding how to develop a meaningful and effective teacher-student relationship. It can be extremely frustrating as you interact with students' attitudes and emotions. The attitudes and emotions are more apparent to teachers at certain grade levels. There will likely be a love-hate relationship with students along the way. At times, you will be loved dearly, and at other times, you might be the most hated person on earth.

The second challenge, covered in Chapter 3, is figuring out the professional behaviors that will help produce the desired outcomes for students. I will share five key focus areas that teachers should incorporate in their daily practice.

A third challenge, which I cover in Chapter 4, is the dilemma of how to set clear expectations and establish consequences. This challenge is important because it is fundamental to having a positive and productive learning environment.

In Chapter 5, I present the fourth challenge regarding the instructional focus in the classroom. This challenge will cover the complexities of managing, understanding, and adapting to students' academic needs. I will share strategies to help address the many aspects of students' academic needs.

The fifth challenge, in Chapter 6, discusses the need to develop deliberate and thoughtful networks to support your work with the students and to support your development as a professional. Many teachers get discouraged because they feel left alone as they are trying to educate students. It is impossible to do it alone.

Chapter 7 will cover the sixth and final challenge teachers need to overcome. This is the challenge of how to develop an effective school-home-community partnership. This area is a struggle for many teachers. Although this challenge is the last one covered, I would suggest that it should be placed very high on the priority list of challenges to overcome.

These six challenges are not all-inclusive by any means. There will be several additional topics discussed within these challenges that could be a separate section or book on their own. To keep you from getting too overwhelmed, these are the six that I will present to you in this book. I realize that teachers deal with so many challenges during the school year and it can lead to the average person becoming discouraged and wanting to leave the profession. I want to encourage you to stay in the race. It is a marathon, not a sprint.

The good news is that you will see steady progress if you stay the course and implement the strategies I am suggesting. You must realize that you only have your students for a limited amount of time and you must make the most of the time that you have with them. If done appropriately, the intense focus needed to implement these strategies will lessen as the school year goes on and as the students get more acclimated.

So be encouraged and know that you can do this. Think about it, there are many other teachers around you that have gone through exactly what you are experiencing. You have some successful role models around you that can provide examples of strategies of success. I suggest that as you read this book, find teachers who are implementing the strategies in this book and see if they are experiencing success. I believe you will find the more strategies they are using effectively, the more likely it is that they are experiencing success.

Also, to help you become even more immersed in the topics I have included an Additional Resources section at the end of the book to provide you with some resources at your fingertips. The resources are only to help you get started with deeper exploration into the topics in the book. It is not intended to be an endorsement of any specific author or concept. You will need to determine the validity of the resources and decide if you agree or disagree with the material that is presented.

So, let's now proceed to the next chapter to discuss the first challenge, which is how to develop effective teacher-student relationships.

Chapter 2

⎯⎯✦⎯⎯

TEACHER-STUDENT
RELATIONSHIPS

This chapter covers an interesting topic. The discussion is focused on how to establish meaningful and effective relationships with your students. I will outline five key points that you should consider when striving to foster a positive and healthy relationship with your students. I would like to remind you that these points are strictly from my perspective.

I should also note that I am sharing my experiences and what "seemed" to have worked for me. I say that with some caution because you never know the total impact your teaching has on your students until either they share their sincere feelings or it is evident in their actions.

Fostering Positive Teacher - Student Relationships: Insights and Key Considerations

There is no exact measuring tool to assess whether you have established a positive relationship with students. So, here we go:

1. Demonstrate Genuine Care for Your Students

This is the foundation that helps to cultivate a solid teacher-student relationship. Students need to know their teachers genuinely care about them as individuals. Showing a sincere commitment to students means that you continue to care for them even when you might not approve of their behavior. It reflects caring about them despite any challenges they may encounter. Truly successful and dedicated teachers will express that they genuinely "love" their students.

Keep in mind this type of love is one that should not violate the professional code of ethics that teachers are sworn to uphold. I will tell you that I had a genuine love for my students. Teachers often assume a parental role, as the students' parents are not present in the classroom. The term "in loco parentis" is used to support teachers' actions when faced with a legal challenge. This term means "in place of the parent." Indeed, you are operating in place of the parent.

Therefore, it is totally acceptable, and expected, that teachers should show a parental kind of love for their students. This means teachers should demonstrate genuine concern for their students in the same way that parents show love for their children. Many teachers think that they are showing they care by allowing students to have what they want despite it not being in the students' best interest.

Demonstrating care for students does not imply that you must always give them what they want. The most effective way to show that you care is to ensure that students receive what they genuinely need. Sometimes, this may lead to them feeling upset, but you will ultimately be on the right side when you prioritize meeting their needs. There are instances when what they need aligns perfectly with what they want-that's when it's a win-win!

Some educators may struggle with this aspect of the relationship. They might grapple with how to show students they care without appearing to cross the line or be excessively lenient. If decisions are made solely to appease students or make them feel good, then you are navigating down the wrong path. Hopefully, the example in the next section will help provide some clarity.

Example: Demonstrate genuine care for students.

Each year that I taught, students often faced personal issues that affected their behavior. Many times, these issues caused them to act out of character, leading to frustration and, at times, disrespect. My approach in any of these situations was to first and foremost communicate to the students that I was concerned about them and their circumstances. I consistently made a distinction between their individual selves and their inappropriate behavior. My care for them remained unwavering, but I did not condone their disrespectful actions. I maintained a mindset that assumed students did not want to be defined by their misconduct.

I distinctly remember one year I was teaching in a school with a high percentage of students receiving free or reduced lunch. There were several days when students arrived at school very hungry. Although the school had a breakfast program, students sometimes came to school after breakfast was over. When the students made it to class they were visibly agitated and would snap at anyone who said anything to them. I learned quickly that a good remedy was to have some extra breakfast items in my classroom to provide to students when they came to school late or just needed a snack. I made a place in the back of my classroom where students could take their snack and eat without interruptions.

As students spent time eating, I always made it a point to check on them and reassure them that I was there to help them settle in. I wanted to make sure they had everything they needed. If the students needed any additional things to be more comfortable, I would take care of it. I also made sure they were aware of what I was teaching in the classroom so they wouldn't feel left out.

My goal was to leave no doubt in their minds that I was in their corner and that I would be there for them regardless of the circumstances. I approached each situation with the assumption that they were grappling with an issue causing them to act out of character. This positive presupposition helped me to have the loving heart that I needed when having a conversation with them. It helped me not to focus on the inappropriate behavior but instead dig deeper to determine the issue that was triggering the behavior. Students seemed to understand and appreciate this approach.

Students recognized that my primary objective was to handle their situations with genuine care and concern. This consistent demonstration of concern helped them understand what it meant to have a teacher who truly cared about them. I believe this created a level of confidence that they needed to be secure in the classroom. This would ultimately help them when they felt vulnerable during academic activities by giving them the comfort they needed to be willing to take risks. As a result, academic achievement increased. That's what we want to see!

2. Put Your Students' Needs First

When you enter the teaching profession, you then take on a responsibility that is greater than most other professions. That's right, teachers are directly or indirectly responsible for the fate of the students they teach. That's a tremendous amount of pressure. Therefore, teachers must consider how all their strategies, decisions, and actions will impact students.

With the responsibility of a teacher being so great, you have no choice but to put your own wants, desires, and needs on the back burner. Yes, you are secondary, and your students are primary. Your students need to be assured that you are a consistent, unwavering, and dependable source. This does not mean that you will cater to their every whim, allow them to do anything they want to do, or let them say whatever they want to say. However, it does mean that you will make it a priority to assure and reassure them that they are your primary focus and you will always do whatever it takes to help them succeed.

Example: Put students' needs first.

I recall a situation when I was teaching that forced me to choose between my desires and students' needs. I had taught a concept in my classroom for several days, creating a variety of activities that I believed effectively reinforced the material. In fact, I thought my preparation and implementation of the lesson plan on this concept were very good.

However, when I graded the assessment during my plan time, I discovered that the scores were similar to previous assessments. My classroom was comprised of a diverse group of learners just like most other classrooms. Therefore, despite my best preparation, a handful of students did not achieve an acceptable score.

My normal procedure was to require the students to get support from myself or a peer who had mastered the concept before they sat for the required retake. My normal process was to provide small group reteaching in class and after school tutoring the day after the assessment. The students would then retake the assessment the following day. So if the initial assessment was on a Wednesday, then the retake would be on a Friday.

After grading this assessment, I compiled a list of students who needed extra support so that I could pull them the following day for small group reteaching. As previously mentioned, a handful of students required more assistance to master the concept. It was a routine process and not outside the norm.

However, the situation became complicated and out of the ordinary when I encountered something unexpected. Here's what happened: I was in my room setting up for my next class when one of my students obtained a pass to come to my class to ask for extra help after school on that same day.

What made the situation complicated is that I had committed to connecting with some colleagues after school to "collaborate" together. Actually, it was going to be more about socializing than anything else. Well, that put me at a crossroad. Do I follow through with my commitment to my colleagues or do I cancel those plans and stay after school with the student?

You wouldn't believe the internal grappling that was taking place. The selfish minions in my mind were trying to convince me that there is no need to stay after because I already had reteaching plans and after school tutoring scheduled for the next day. Those little minions argued that I should honor my commitment to my colleagues and that since the student hadn't given me prior notice, it was acceptable to decline the request for after school support.

Yet I also had some caring thoughts reminding me that I should stay with the student because tomorrow is not promised to anyone, so I needed to act today. I MUST honor my promise to all my students from the beginning: that I would be there for them when they needed me. You can't place time parameters on students' needs; you must adopt a "right now" mindset.

Needless to say, I ultimately put my own plans on the backburner and decided to stay after school to support the student. There will be times when there might be schedule conflicts, competing events, or just sometimes not having a desire or the will to be available. It is important that your normal professional practice is to put students' needs first.

This is not to say that you won't need to recharge by engaging in activities for yourself at some point. You shouldn't feel guilty about that. Taking care of your morale and physical well-being is very important. At the end of the day, doing so will make you an even better teacher.

3. Be the teacher

You might say this is common sense and that you don't need to waste any time talking about it. However, common sense is not so common anymore. So, let's dive a little deeper into this point. Many teachers base their decisions, actions, and comments on whether they think their students will like them or not. As a teacher, the primary responsibility is to manage every situation in the classroom from the perspective of a professional who is responsible and accountable for the academic outcomes of your students. Therefore, you must take charge of the classroom and act accordingly.

You don't need to seek the approval or happiness of your students when making decisions in your classroom. You are not their friend or peer. Some teachers make a huge mistake when they allow the interactions with their students to feel like a friendly relationship. Don't misunderstand me; it is okay-and even advisable-to be nice to your students. However, it is not acceptable for them to view you as their equal. You can be nice and firm at the same time. It is definitely a great situation when your students are happy with your decisions, but that should not be the driving force when making a decision. You should avoid allowing the lines in the teacher-student relationship to become blurred. Say what you mean and mean what you say.

Example: Being the teacher.

I recall quite a few instances during my teaching career when students would mention what other teachers were doing in their classroom. They would spend some time trying to convince me that I should allow them to have the same "fun" in my classroom as their other teachers allowed. I would always listen to their stories and sometimes ask follow-up questions to see if their suggestions were reasonable. It was astonishing how even students who hadn't had those teachers would chime in to agree with their peers.

However, in most cases the students never included any academics in what they were explaining to me. It was always nonacademic activities such as watching a music video, listening to music, or drawing pictures. You can probably imagine what they would say when I asked them what they wanted to do in my classroom. Yes, the answers were very similar to the activities they described from the other teachers' classrooms. It did not take long to realize that if I allowed students to be the decision-makers regarding classroom activities they would rarely, if ever, choose academic work.

I also realized that students didn't always provide an accurate account of what happened in their other classrooms. In fact, their accounts were often inaccurate when they were trying to get what they wanted. I don't recall them ever suggesting that I teach them about an important topic in the textbook instead of allowing them some "free time" to chat with their friends. You have probably had similar experiences with your students. I predict that if you allowed your students to decide what they should do in the classroom each day, they would choose non-academic activities as well.

As the teacher, I was charged with making decisions that were in the best interest of my students, regardless of whether they agreed with or liked those decisions. Here's how I handled these situations: When students suggested we should have "fun" instead of doing academic work, I would note all the activities they suggested. I would then explain that if I allowed those activities instead of covering the academic material, I would be disregarding the expectations placed on me by the school district, my principal, and their parents.

I would then ask them to give me some suggestions on what I could tell the district office, my principal and their parents when they found out that they weren't learning anything. A popular comment from a student would be, "They won't know." I would remind students that they would likely share with other teachers what we did the same way they have shared with me what the other teachers did in their classroom. I would also let the students know that everyone would find out when they saw the assessment scores.

As I waited for students to provide me with some brilliant responses I could use to explain why they weren't learning, I shared that their actions could jeopardize my job; I could be fired if I allowed them to continuously engage in non-academic activities. Needless to say, I did not receive many logical responses that I could use to justify what they wanted.

Therefore, my decision was to move forward with the academics I had planned. However, I would let the students know that I would allow them to choose from one of the activities they suggested if they mastered the concept I was teaching before the end of the time I allotted to teach it. Usually that created extra motivation for them to be more attentive and engaged.

The primary message is that I had to be the teacher in charge, explain the consequences involved in the situation, and then make decisions that were in the best interest of my students. If I had allowed students to have what they initially wanted, they would have enjoyed some short-term happiness. However, the long-term consequences would have been much more detrimental. Therefore, teachers "must" accept their role and take appropriate actions to fulfill their obligation as the teacher.

4. Establish Open and Honest Two-Way Communication

Yes, you might say this is another common-sense point, but I believe it is a very powerful and necessary aspect to consider when establishing and maintaining a healthy relationship with your students. While you have the clear rights and authority as a teacher to make decisions in the best interest of your students, this authority is not intended to create a dictatorship. You can take the stance that what you say is the first and last word in all situations.

However, that position will likely lead to unintended adverse consequences that may cause damage you may not be able to repair. Therefore, it is important to use good diplomacy and work through situations in a manner that gives your students some input. You may have heard the old proverb, "An ounce of prevention is worth a pound of cure." Allowing students to have input may just be that ounce of prevention that helps avoid a major student revolt.

The two-way communication process not only provides insight into your students' perspective but also gives you an opportunity to share your thoughts and rationale from a teacher's perspective. You do have the authority to make the final decision, but the decision will be more secure if you have some insight into how your students feel and think about the situation. I must admit that this can be a difficult method to master when you are wrestling with the feelings and thoughts of a classroom of students. However, exercising patience will help coupled with the assurance that you ultimately have the final decision.

A good relationship becomes a great one when you can be empathetic during the interactions and decision-making process. It is very unlikely you will be empathetic if you never allow students to share in the conversation as you contemplate a decision. Deciding without any input is the easiest way to go, but it might be the hardest thing for your students to accept.

Example: Establish open and honest two-way communication.

When I started teaching, I was told that I needed to maintain complete control of my classroom by establishing rules that students needed to follow. To me, this meant I needed to create a list of classroom rules that all students had to obey. That was the mindset I had going into my first year of teaching.

I spent quite a bit of time contemplating the rules I wanted to use in my classroom. As a rule came to me, I wrote it down. Before I knew it I had about 13 rules that I knew would help me to have complete control in the classroom. I thought the number 13 was an odd number so I cut it back to 12. Yes, a dozen rules sounded like a good round number and then I could come up with a cool name like "The Daily Dozen." It was more like "The Daily Don'ts" because the majority of the rules told students what not to do such as:

- Don't talk while I'm talking.

- Don't get out of your seat without permission.

- Don't throw things.

- Don't yell in the classroom.

- Don't say mean things to others.

- Don't.......

I won't list them all because I think you get the point. My list was full of prohibitions. Remember, I felt this was important to have control of my classroom. Well, the students didn't respond as I imagined they would. I knew I would get some resistance but I wasn't prepared for the reactions I received. Let's take a look at what actually happened.

On the first day of school, I spent the class period going over my rules and making sure the students understood them. I didn't get many questions about the rules so I assumed all the students had a good understanding of my rules. However, it did not take long for the students to start trying to outsmart me regarding the rules.

I saw one student throw a pencil to another student. When I addressed it, the student insisted that the pencil was "tossed" not "thrown." Another situation occurred when I noticed two students talking while I was teaching. When I pointed out the rule violation, one of the students said they were not "talking" they were "whispering."

After constantly putting out fires in that manner, I determined that I needed to do things differently. The negative tone that I set with the rules could not be sustained for an entire school year. Therefore, I decided to hit the reset button. My new plan was to go to the students, admit that I had taken the wrong approach and let them know we needed to start over.

It was a Monday morning about mid-September. I opened each class by telling my students how disappointed I was with the way I set up the rules for my classroom. I then told them that I had taken their thoughts and feelings for granted and I wanted to make amends. I told them that realized I had established "my" classroom rules for "our" classroom. I told them I would write down their suggestions so that they could see their ideas in writing.

I stated that "we" need to establish "our" classroom guidelines to ensure that we all feel comfortable in the classroom each day. I could see the students becoming more relaxed. I could also feel the tension easing up as I was speaking.

I then opened the conversation to allow students to give their input on what they thought good guidelines would be for our classroom. I reassured them that they could be honest without any repercussions. As a result, we changed from "rules" to "expectations" since I concluded from their comments that "rules" created an authoritarian tone. We also removed "don't" from all the statements because they shared that it felt like they couldn't do anything in the classroom because of the way the statements were worded.

As students shared their thoughts, I also had to remind them to listen to each other while they were sharing. We had a very lively conversation, and it helped create an environment where they felt respected and heard. I also knew I had to consider that each student might have their own ideas of what would work in the classroom.

We ended up with a much shorter list of general expectations that could apply to a wide range of behaviors. The result was fewer items, a positive tone, collaborative conversation, and total student buy-in. That was just one example of having open and honest communication with the students. I used this method on most decisions either individually with a student or collectively with the class.

The impact of allowing students to have input was amazing. My classroom transformed into a place where students felt ownership and pride, and our interactions became much more productive. They started holding each other accountable when someone didn't follow the classroom expectations. I saw a shift in my authority, where it was no longer a power struggle between teacher and student. Instead, it became a shared responsibility for the classroom.

5. Be Adaptable

The role of a teacher is very difficult. Many would argue that it's more demanding today than ever before. Students' perceptions of their teachers evolve as they spend more time in the classroom, and their attitudes can shift based on various situations. To build and sustain a positive relationship with students, you must be adaptable. There is a constant need to adjust to how you connect with each one of them. Initially, students are often assessing if they can trust you to be reliable and supportive. Gaining their trust is a major milestone, as it sets the foundation for a meaningful teacher-student relationship.

However, even when they completely trust you there will be moments when their attitudes might shift in a direction that can be hard to explain. These shifts might be influenced by factors beyond the classroom, such as hormonal changes, peer influences, or external circumstances. When these changes occur, you may notice unusual behaviors or strained interactions with certain students. Therefore, it is critical to adapt to the swings in behavior so you can keep the relationship moving in a positive direction.

Students are unique individuals with different personalities and life circumstances, so adjusting how you approach each relationship is crucial. Being adaptable also means remaining honest with them about what you believe is best for their success in any given situation. Often, students may feel they know what's best for themselves, but as their teacher, you have the responsibility to guide them thoughtfully. Let me share an example of how I adapted my approach to accommodate the individual needs of my students while maintaining a fair and respectful environment.

Example: Demonstrating Adaptability.

Adapting to changes in my relationships with each student was essential, and it extended to accommodating their individual differences. This meant I couldn't treat each student exactly the same, despite my commitment to a fair and consistent standard. Fairness sometimes looks different in practice, requiring nuanced approaches to meet the unique needs of each student.

When I collected assignments from the class, I noticed that this particular student hadn't submitted his work. I had already received an email from his parent regarding her frustration when trying to motivate him to complete the assignment. I approached him to discuss the missing assignment, giving him the opportunity to explain. Rather than disclosing the major conflict he had with his parent he simply told me he had forgotten. From my past interactions with this student and his family, I knew he often felt embarrassed when I brought up personal matters, especially those his parent shared with me.

Understanding his situation, I chose not to reprimand him or issue an automatic failing grade. Instead, I adapted my response to show understanding and support. I recognized that his parent's involvement, while well-meaning, had played a role in the missed deadline, making it appropriate to help him devise a solution. Together, we discussed ways he could complete and submit the assignment. We also talked about how he might manage his responsibilities to prevent similar situations in the future. As a result, he was able to complete the assignment quickly after our conversation.

My approach to avoid scolding the student for missing the assignment deadline, discuss ways to help him complete and submit the assignment, and have the conversation about options to consider in the future created a much better outcome. It also gave the student some problem-solving strategies that would be valuable in future situations.

I believe this approach helped to strengthen our relationship because the student was reassured that I was considering his personal situation rather than focusing only on the assignment. As the situations required, I made the necessary adaptation that was in the student's best interest. This was my mindset when I interacted with my students.

Developing a unique plan tailored to each student's needs is challenging and requires careful, consistent handling. You don't need to know every detail of their private lives, but understanding the key aspects that impact their school experience is essential. This understanding allows you to proactively anticipate potential issues and be prepared with constructive solutions. By building these insights, you'll be able to respond to challenges effectively and maintain a positive relationship with your students-even when obstacles arise.

This approach should help you to be much more proactive with your strategy. If you know ahead of time about the things that will potentially cause a strain on your relationship, it gives you more insight to make better decisions and have solutions already available when issues come up. *Because issues WILL come up.*

In summary, you should now be aware of some strategies that will help you to develop and maintain an effective teacher-student relationship.

You must be intentional with the five points in the relationship building process. To reiterate what I have shared, you need to:

- Show your students that you care,

- Commit to putting your students' needs first,

- Commit to being the teacher,

- Establish open and honest two-way communication, and

- Be adaptable.

Chapter 3 will delve deeper into building on this foundation, focusing on specific traits that enhance your professional practice. I will share some key areas I believe teachers should prioritize when working with their students.

Chapter 3

FIVE FOCUS AREAS

I t is very important to focus on areas in your professional practice that will make you a great educator. In other words, there are some fundamental practices that I believe are important for teachers to consistently practice that will help when working with students in the classroom.

In today's school environment, it seems to be more challenging for educators to do the right thing. There is so much public scrutiny surrounding even the most basic professional practices. The challenges teachers are facing seem to have caused teachers to become uncertain about many situations during their daily encounters. For this reason, it is essential that educators remain steadfast and resist the negative external pressures prevalent in society.

While this is easier said than done, the relentless scrutiny can feel overwhelming. It often seems that everyone has an opinion on how teachers should handle their work. Social media is filled with so-called "educational experts" eager to offer unsolicited advice, with controversial ideas quickly gaining traction.

Politicians, too, contribute by enacting laws that restrict teachers' behaviors, often based on the preferences of influential donors rather than the insights of experienced educators. Oftentimes politicians are driven by the opinions of their largest individual or group donors and not by those in the school setting who have the most insight.

Businesses exert their influence on schools, believing their views should be prioritized since they may eventually hire graduates. Therefore, they are sometimes very aggressive in their demands on teachers. The individuals in these businesses tend to forget that they had effective teachers who helped provide them with the educational foundation they have acquired.

The media plays a vital role in creating a narrative that may create a more difficult environment for teachers. Reporters can often take the words of a bystander or community member and make it seem as though that opinion is accurate. They seldom state a disclaimer to let the public know that the information may not be accurate or factual. Therefore, people might then start repeating inaccurate information about how teachers should work with their students.

These are a few of the negative forces in our society that make teachers very cautious about their practice. No one wants to be scrutinized to the extent that it makes them afraid to take care of their basic professional responsibilities. However, I want to believe there is still hope that our teachers can push past all of the negative forces and become outstanding educators.

I continue to hold onto the belief that educators can overcome these obstacles and continue to excel in their profession. When you practice something enough it becomes a habit. When it becomes a habit then you do it without even thinking about it.

Some people subscribe to the saying that practice makes perfect. My thought is that perfect practice makes perfect. It is easy to practice bad behavior. If you do, then you will get perfect bad habits. With this line of thinking, I suggest five professional practices that teachers should turn into habits.

As I contemplated which professional practices were most important, I spent time reflecting on the practices I noticed along the way that yielded the best results. I must say that I engaged in a lot of practices beyond the ones that I am sharing here. Also, it is not a matter of whether a teacher does or does not engage in these practices, but it is more about gauging to what extent they are shown.

Reflecting on the methods I found most effective, I identified five essential professional practices, summarized in the acronym "CHEER": Commitment, Honesty, Empathy, Education, and Reflection. I will spend some time discussing the importance of each one of these and what these practices look like when they are implemented. Through my teaching experience and observations as an administrator, I have seen the impact of these values firsthand.

1. Commitment

Commitment involves being wholly engaged-physically, mentally, and emotionally. There are many teachers in our schools but the numbers decrease, in some cases drastically, when you identify the ones who are physically, mentally, and emotionally committed.

For example, a teacher can be described as committed because of a stellar attendance record. I have witnessed teachers who never miss a day of school. It is admirable for a teacher to have that type of consistency. We should all agree that students need their teachers to be present consistently. This is a basic level of commitment that does not meet my definition. Simply showing up without the right mindset or emotional connection will not get the best results.

For instance, a teacher might have perfect attendance but approach each day with a negative attitude, leading to poor student interactions, increased disciplinary actions, and low morale. This is the primary reason I believe commitment must go beyond just being physically present. We need to include the added components of mental and emotional engagement to get the best results.

Teachers who embody this level of commitment demonstrate it in ways that are easily recognized by students, colleagues, and parents alike. When I was a building administrator I would take time to reflect on the teachers who had the best results in their classroom to see what they were doing that made them successful. In my experience as a school administrator, the most committed teachers displayed several common traits.

The teachers with the highest level of commitment would make the time to get the job done, whatever the job might be. This would include lesson preparation, grading papers, collaboration with colleagues, contacting parents, or gathering resources. Time was not a factor for the successful teachers.

They also would never stop thinking about what they needed to do to be at their best. They were always mentally engaged. It was not unusual for one of these highly committed teachers to send me a text or stop by my office to share an epiphany with me. When the mental light bulb lit up they would share their thought with great enthusiasm.

Another common finding from observing these teachers was that they displayed an intense passion. They were emotionally committed to the work and their students. When they had an idea that they felt would improve their teaching or their students' situations they would passionately share it. This level of passion would often spill over to colleagues. That could be good or bad. It all depends on the way it was displayed. In my experience, if a teacher's motives are pure then the emotions attached to their actions usually work out for the best.

Teachers who practice high levels of commitment are physically, mentally, and emotionally present each day. It does not mean that some days one or two areas of their commitment might not be at its peak. For these teachers those times will be the exception rather than the norm. It is a great sight to see when teachers have a maximum level of commitment. This is when students will likely get the best education.

2. Honesty

Honesty is being truthful in all situations to the best of your ability even when it might be uncomfortable or unpopular. Honesty has become an obscure concept in our society. However, I do believe there is still hope. To make honesty a more familiar concept it will take some work and determination. It is so easy not to be honest that many people don't think twice about whether they should be honest or not. People can do and say some things that are dishonest.

I should also point out that sometimes the things people don't say or do can make them dishonest as well. In other words, there may be some valuable information that a teacher omits when explaining a situation involving a student or colleague. Intentionally leaving out an important detail that could make a difference in the final decision is a form of dishonesty.

Usually when someone is being dishonest, it is about self-preservation. People tend to do whatever is necessary to avoid getting in trouble. We often see this with students but it is also prevalent with adults. You might have experienced examples of dishonesty with your students or colleagues. If you have not then you are either living through a miraculous situation or your head is stuck in the sand.

Since dishonesty is so prevalent, I suggest that there needs to be an intentional effort to practice being honest. Honesty does not come naturally. Therefore, teachers must make it a priority in their practice.

Students, parents, administrators, and community members must be able to trust teachers. I stressed this practice both as a teacher myself and as an administrator supervising teachers.

I recall many situations where honesty played a major part of the outcome. One situation specifically stands out. When I was serving as building principal, I received a call from a parent who was upset because her child was told he could not attend a school dance. The teacher had communicated to the parent that the student had not met the criteria of completing all missed assignments.

I placed the parent on hold and contacted the teacher to see if it was true that the student had not turned in the assignment. The teacher told me that the student was not eligible to attend the dance because of his failure to turn in the missed assignments. I then went back and told the parent that the teacher was following the guidelines and the student could not attend the dance.

The parent proceeded to tell me that she had personally witnessed her child do the assignments and had him turn them in. At this point, my mind started churning because there had been instances in the past where situations got a bit messy because of some details that were not shared. I decided to go back to the teacher to ask again about the student's situation.

The teacher then shared with me that the student had turned in the assignments but they had not been graded. The teacher also told me that the team felt that it was best that the student did not attend the dance because he was likely to cause a disturbance. I shared with the teacher that since the assignments were turned in that we would have to allow the student to attend the school dance and the behavior concerns should be addressed in a different manner.

I then called the parent and told her that her child would be able to attend the school dance. I also told her that the team and I needed her to let her child know the behavior expectations he needed to follow. She assured me that she would work with her child. Before we ended the conversation, the parent told me that she would be willing to attend the school dance to make sure her child followed the behavior expectations. Without hesitation I agreed to this option. It ended up being a positive experience for the student.

This situation was a case of a teacher not being completely honest with me. The teacher knew the missing assignments had been submitted but there was important information left out that I could have used from the beginning of the conversation. I believe the teacher was trying to help make the dance a success by eliminating a potential disruption, but it was not the right approach.

If the teacher had practiced honesty correctly, then all the information would have been shared initially. This would have helped us avoid having to address the upset parent. The student would have been spared the initial disappointment of being denied the opportunity to attend the school dance. Also, I would not have had to spend the extra time on this situation.

Being completely honest is not always easy. Sometimes it is really hard. However, not being completely honest can have a negative impact on students. The goal as teachers should always be to practice behaviors that create a positive impact on our students, parents, and colleagues.

3. Empathy

Empathy is the ability to understand the experiences of others by imagining yourself being in a similar situation. This concept may be one that is most difficult for teachers to practice. One might ask why it is so difficult to grasp. Well, a major part of it is that most people are naturally self-centered. Empathy means that you can acknowledge, understand, or relate to the emotions of others as you formulate an opinion about them or their situation.

Empathy is a critical and necessary component of the decision-making process when the decisions being made will have an impact on the lives of others. Based on the many years I have interacted with people, I have concluded that people struggle to consider the needs of others ahead of, or even alongside, their own.

In my experience, I have found that teachers struggle with the concept of empathy just like everybody else. I noticed this throughout my interactions in schools as an educator, administrator, and in the community as a citizen. That is why I believe it is important for teachers to intentionally model and practice this concept when interacting with students.

There are many specific examples I can share that will give you a very clear picture of the importance of practicing empathy. Rather than go into an example of a particular situation, I will share with you the way that I monitored my actions as a teacher and a supervisor of teachers. My strategy was to ask myself some questions that would help me to better connect with students and their feelings. I would ask:

- How would I want to be treated if this was a situation I had to face?

- How would I feel if someone was treating me this way?

- What would my response be if I had to respond to this situation?

- If this was my child, how would I feel about this situation?

- How would I have felt if my teachers treated me this way or allowed this to happen to me when I was a student?

- What feelings or situations did I experience that I don't want my students to ever experience?

- How is this situation impacting the student's feeling of self-confidence and self-worth?

- How is this situation impacting the way others feel about this student?

These questions are primarily designed to help understand how students are feeling during any given situation. Empathy is practiced best when you can truly understand how other people feel during a particular situation.

The list of questions I have presented includes an attempt to help teachers understand the feelings as if they were the parent or the student. There is also an attempt to help teachers consider the feelings of the student's classmates. You can guarantee that the students who are affected will focus on how their friends are feeling about them or what they think about them at that moment.

I believe it is very important for teachers to remember that situations students go through have an impact on more than just the individual student. In addition to the student's feelings, parents and classmates will have an emotional investment as well. Therefore, it makes it more important to practice empathy during all situations.

Throughout the years, I have not always been able to be as empathetic as I needed to be. I am going to guess that you haven't either. I will also say that you probably won't always be as empathetic as you need to be in future situations. That is just reality. However, I will ask that you be intentional with how you approach future situations.

Make it part of your routine practice to ask yourself some questions that help you tap into the feelings of others. Contemplate whether you are going about your work in an empathetic manner. Make changes if you aren't. If you are, continue doing what you're doing. I believe this approach will be an effective way to prioritize empathy into your regular practice as an educator.

4. Education

Education is the knowledge you must have to effectively teach your students. To maximize this focus area, I believe teachers must focus on two parts of their education. Teachers must be educated in their content area and educated on how to teach their content to the students. This means it is about both the content and pedagogy.

First, teachers should be thoroughly educated in their content area. Not having a sound education in the content area can cause significant problems in the classroom. Teachers who do not have a thorough understanding of their content area can cause students to suffer academically. If this happens then it will create more challenges for students as they continue their journey through school.

The second part of the focus on education is pedagogy. Teachers must be well educated on how to best teach the content to the students. It is necessary to understand how students learn, the best way to present the content, and the resources needed to maximize the effectiveness of the lesson. Many teachers believe it is about teaching good lessons that determine their effectiveness. However, I believe it is primarily about how much students are learning that determines a teacher's effectiveness.

The best way teachers can increase their education in both content and pedagogy is to engage in ongoing professional development (PD). That's right PD. To some teachers, just the mere mention of PD will cause them to run the other way. Some teachers must be forced to go to PD sessions while kicking and screaming along the way. Trust me, I understand that sentiment because I have also experienced some PD that made me want to pluck my eyeballs out.

Let me go a bit deeper into PD and how it can work to your advantage. PD in its true form should be designed to improve teachers' knowledge base either in content or pedagogy. Although there are many PD topics that do not directly address content or pedagogy, I suggest that they all directly or indirectly impact these two areas. My conclusion is that all PD, when done correctly, either helps you know what to teach or how best to teach it or sometimes both.

Therefore, teachers should go into PD with a positive mindset and a determination to come out of it with more education either on what to teach or how to best teach the content. I am a firm believer that you get what you expect. If you expect to get nothing out of a PD session, you likely will be right. Therefore, it is important to go into a PD session to expect at least one thing you can use in your professional practice. You have then improved your education.

PD can be sponsored by school buildings, district offices, or professional associations. It can also be in the form of individual college courses or degree programs. PD can be taken online or onsite at a designated location. Regardless of who sponsors it or how it is offered, it is important for teachers to engage in ongoing PD.

As I stated, I believe ongoing PD should be an essential part of teachers' professional practice. However, I believe there are a few specific ways teachers can approach PD to maximize its effectiveness and thus increase their level of content education and pedagogy. I want to share a two-step approach to how I have been able to maximize the impact of PD in my practice. Step one is about the PD itself and step two is about the teacher's mindset and actions.

The first step is to participate in PD that does the following:

- Addresses a personal weakness.

- Relates to your student population.

- Aligns with a learning format that works best for you (i.e., online vs. in-person, in-building vs. other location, etc.).

- Leads to a certificate or degree.

- Strengthens your pedagogy by focusing on student individuality (i.e., poverty, learning styles, differentiation, etc.).

This is a critical step toward getting you much closer to having the desired level of education you need as a teacher.

The next step, and perhaps the most important, is having the right mindset about the PD. This is very critical. To maximize the PD experience, teachers must:

- Go into it with positive expectations.

- Be empathetic toward the speaker.

- Be intentional to get at least one concept or activity to take with you.

- Be determined to incorporate something you learned into your practice immediately.

- Teach what you learned to colleagues.

These are some important practices that will help develop habits that should increase teacher effectiveness.

This two-part list is not all-inclusive, but it does give teachers some essential practices that should yield positive results if they are done consistently. The overall goal is to have a higher level of education in your content and a better understanding of how to best teach the content to your students. It is my belief that approaching PD in the manner I have described will help you to achieve that goal.

5. Reflection

Reflection is the process of analyzing one's own actions. As I define reflection, it is not only analyzing one's own actions but it is also making behavioral changes as a result. An analysis alone merely provides information. A person must honestly assess the information and determine how to respond. Reflection can be the most useful practice if it is done correctly.

The concept of teachers becoming reflective practitioners is nothing new. Since the start of my teaching career, I have had mentors and colleagues talk about this concept. When teachers engage in reflection it should lead to an improvement in practice.

Reflection is not always a natural or automatic thing to do. I believe teachers must intentionally incorporate reflection into their practice. That means carving out time to analyze your actions and situations to determine what happened and how your practice should change moving forward.

During the reflection process, teachers should not only consider their own perspective, but they should also think about the perspectives of students, parents, colleagues, community members, and administrators. Regardless of the situation, there is an opportunity to think about how things will impact others. Keeping all these perspectives in mind during reflection helps to broaden the scope of the analysis.

My process of reflection over the years has become more thoughtful and intentional. Early in my career, I was much more conscious of my own feelings and needs. As I matured and had more experiences my mindset shifted to a broader analysis process. I must admit it was not an easy transition. My selfish nature wanted to be the predominant force. However, along the way I was motivated to expand my reflective analysis to include the perspective of others. It made all the difference in how I adjusted my practice and most importantly how I felt.

I will share my reflection process so that you have an idea of what worked well for me. Keep in mind that you may not completely agree with my process so feel free to adjust as you deem necessary. It is mainly a focus on having a broad scope when analyzing situations. In some cases your reflection process may be broader than mine. That's totally fine. I certainly do not claim to have mastered this process. My time both as a teacher and leader of teachers was filled with situations that did not go the way I expected. Therefore, I had to engage in some deep reflection to determine what went wrong and how to have a better outcome moving forward.

My process was intentional in two ways. First, I made sure I set aside some time in a private space to engage in reflection. Second, I asked myself a series of questions about the situation.

The first part of my reflection process, which is setting aside reflection time, is not too complicated. I simply put reflection in my daily schedule to guarantee I would engage in the process. I also let others know that I was not to be disturbed during this time. Students, colleagues, and even my family members eventually learned not to interrupt me when I was engaging in my reflection. They came to understand how much of a priority I placed on reflection. As I became more consistent and intentional, it became very easy to spend quality time in reflection.

The second part of my reflection process, which is contemplating a series of questions, helped me get to the heart of the situation. This part provided me with some valuable information that I could use to impact my practice. The following questions are the basic questions I usually include in my reflection process.

- Was the overall objective accomplished?

- Did this situation go exactly as I planned?

- What are some reasons it did not go as planned?

- How did my actions impact others?

- What were some verbal or nonverbal communication cues I should have noticed?

- Did I communicate exactly as I should have?

- Who do I need to contact to correct any misunderstandings?

- How could I have done things differently in this situation?

- What changes do I need to make to get better results in the future?

There were always additional questions that were specific to a given situation, but I felt these questions helped me get to the core of the matter at hand. After answering these questions I felt much better about what happened and how to do things differently the next time. It was sometimes painful to be honest with myself. I believe being true to myself is what helped me to grow. The more I intentionally practiced this concept the easier it became to focus on the issue. For me, that was a great way to improve my professional practice. I suggest it will work for you as well.

In this chapter, I have shared five focus areas that teachers should intentionally incorporate in their professional practice. Commitment, Honesty, Empathy, Education, and Reflection (CHEER) are very important areas that should become habits as teachers strive to become effective educators. I believe the teachers who constantly improve their professional practice in these areas will get better achievement results with their students.

In the next chapter, we will focus more specifically within the classroom. Chapter 4 addresses how teachers should set expectations and issue consequences when students don't meet those expectations.

Chapter 4

———————— ❧❧❧ ————————

SETTING EXPECTATIONS AND CONSEQUENCES

T his chapter focuses on strategies teachers can use to set expectations
for their students and implement consequences when those
expectations are not met. Establishing expectations is a proactive process
while implementing consequences is reactive. Both processes require
careful planning and intentionality.

Teachers must prioritize setting expectations for their students while
acknowledging that not every student will adhere to them perfectly. As
such, having a structured set of consequences ready to enforce is essential.
In the next sections, I will share some insight on ways teachers should
approach both setting expectations and implementing consequences.

Expectations

To begin, it is essential to clarify what is meant by "setting expectations."
This refers to the process of defining guidelines for the desired student
behaviors in the classroom. It involves clearly articulating acceptable
actions and, in some cases, identifying prohibited ones. In essence, this

process establishes how everyone in the classroom, including the teacher, will interact and operate.

Another way to frame it is that you are setting the behavioral norms and patterns that create the classroom culture. This foundational step is key to fostering an environment that is respectful, peaceful, engaging, and fun. The expectations you establish should reflect the kind of atmosphere you aim to cultivate.

When I approached this process, I always ensured that the expectations were age appropriate. It is important to differentiate between expectations for the teacher (as the adult) and those for the students. While some behaviors are universal, adults should not be expected to act like children, and vice versa.

However, this does not mean that teachers can't play and act childish sometimes. It may be a time when that may be the appropriate behavior when building relationships with the students. It also does not mean that children can't display adult-like maturity in certain situations. That may be appropriate as well.

Students thrive in environments with consistent, predictable expectations that are routinely enforced. Initially, students may need more leeway to make mistakes, but over time, they should develop habits that align with the established expectations.

I typically categorized my expectations into two areas: general classroom norms and routines/procedures. For the former, I encouraged student input to foster a sense of ownership, whereas the latter were predetermined before students entered the classroom.

General Classroom Norms

Based on my past experiences and through extensive research, I am convinced that there are some basic guidelines to consider when establishing general classroom norms. Unfortunately, I made a few mistakes along the way to gain the understanding I have now. I would like to save other teachers the trouble by sharing a list of points to consider when establishing classroom norms. You might consider the following points.

1. Classroom norms should be written to state what you want students to do.

Teachers often focus on what they don't want students to do, creating rules filled with "don'ts." This approach can unintentionally set a negative tone, discouraging students, and hindering their openness to learning.

The goal of any classroom should be to create a positive and safe learning environment. Doing so will increase the likelihood that students will develop and maintain an open mind to learn. Therefore, being intentional about the language you use in the classroom norms is very important.

A valuable resource I have found is Positive Behavioral Interventions and Supports (PBIS). PBIS emphasizes positive reinforcement to create a safe and supportive learning environment, offering strategies that have consistently proven effective for me and could benefit other educators as well.

2. Classroom norms should be general enough to cover a wide range of specific behaviors.

Many teachers attempt to address specific behaviors in their norms, resulting in an unwieldy list. This not only makes the norms difficult to manage but also creates loopholes, as students may argue that unlisted behaviors do not warrant consequences. In my experience, classroom norms that are general will provide the teacher with much more leverage. Teachers should be thoughtful in their planning to create words that capture a wide range of behaviors. As a result, there will be less time wasted on trying to determine which general norm applies to the specific behavior being addressed.

Broadly worded norms provide greater flexibility for teachers. By thoughtfully selecting terms that encompass a wide range of behaviors, teachers can address issues more efficiently. For example, having a norm "to be respectful" covers various undesirable behaviors, such as name-calling, interrupting, or making fun of others. Using such encompassing language allows teachers to respond effectively to many situations without needing an exhaustive list.

3. Classroom norms should be aligned with the school's norms.

Teachers need to set up their classroom norms so that they support the overall building norms. Students tend to behave much better with consistency. Norms should be consistent across classrooms and throughout all areas in the school building. This does not mean they must be exactly the same. However, classroom norms and building norms should not contradict each other.

Although an easy solution would be to have building and classroom norms the same, that is usually not the case. I have not worked in a school where that is the situation. In most instances, teachers have the autonomy to develop a set of classroom norms that works best for their students. I believe this is the best approach for school buildings.

One practical way to ensure alignment is by prominently displaying school norms in the classroom and referring to them regularly. This consistency benefits students, teachers, and administrators alike.

4. Students should be allowed to have input.

Student input is essential when establishing classroom norms. As you probably have already noticed, students typically have a lot of opinions. Giving them an opportunity to be heard is very important. It helps student morale, their sense of belonging, and their feeling of self-worth.

If students help create the classroom norms, they are more likely to honor them. After all, they now have some ownership in the norms. That usually leads to more student buy-in. When that happens then they become extra enforcers on your behalf. They don't want anybody to violate "their norms."

Another reason student input is important is that they can't point fingers at the teacher if the norms don't seem to be working for the class. If things are not working with the norms, the teacher can't be the scapegoat because the norms were created with class input and agreement.

Hopefully, this helps you understand the importance of allowing student input in creating classroom norms. Using this strategy helps students feel better about the norms and helps minimize or possibly eliminate animosity toward the teacher.

5. Classroom norms should not exceed four or five items.

This is something that I could have woven into a previous point. However, I believe it is important enough to be listed on its own. Teachers should be very careful not to have too many classroom norms. If teachers include words that capture a wide range of behaviors there will be no need to have a lot of norms.

By nature, teachers like to provide a lot of details to their students. However, this is not the area to be verbose. It may seem counterintuitive, but less is more in this instance. When there are fewer general statements, teachers have more discretion in controlling the interpretation. Classrooms operate much better when the teacher is in control. Go figure!

Let me share an example of a set of classroom norms that I have seen to be very effective. There were three items: 1) Be safe, 2) Be respectful, and 3) Be responsible. These norms capture most behaviors that happen in any classroom. I feel a teacher can fold any behavior into one of these norms. These norms address classroom safety and etiquette, thus promoting a safe and positive learning environment. That's the goal!

Classroom Routines

Classroom routines should focus on the varied and recurring scenarios that students encounter daily in the classroom. Unlike classroom norms, classroom routines need to be explicitly defined and highly specific. This provides teachers with an opportunity to establish the structured environment students require to self-regulate their behavior effectively. Clear and concise directions significantly enhance student outcomes. In contrast, if students are left to form their own interpretations of what is expected, chaos is likely to ensue.

To minimize such disorder, teachers should thoughtfully develop routines that address a broad spectrum of daily classroom interactions. Let us explore the essential elements of effective classroom routines and the components teachers might incorporate. Effective classroom routines should cover the following aspects:

- Entering the classroom at the beginning of class

- Exiting the classroom at the end of class

- Assignment submission process

- Whether getting up is at the student's discretion or teacher permission must be granted first

- Process for asking and answering questions

- Group work process that includes defined roles

- Safety procedures for any labs or activities

- Passing out and collecting materials

- Permission to leave the classroom (restroom, locker, nurse, etc.)

- Answering the door when someone knocks

- Answering the classroom telephone when someone calls

- Personal emergencies

- Classroom or building emergencies (physical altercations, fire drills, etc.)

This is by no means an exhaustive list. Some teachers may find it necessary to expand or condense their routines based on the unique needs of their classroom. There is no magic formula for creating a perfectly smooth classroom environment. The overarching goal is to anticipate potential areas of confusion and provide students with clear, consistent instructions to prevent disruptive behaviors.

There are a few critical steps teachers need to take to ensure the routines work as intended. Developing classroom routines is only the beginning of the process. There are a few more things teachers need to do regarding the routines. If teachers merely develop the routines and post them, it would be just another poster that students pass by every day.

Below are five steps teachers can follow to ensure that their classroom routines are embraced, internalized, and consistently followed. These steps are not presented in order of priority, as each plays an equally significant role. Teachers should avoid cutting corners to save time, as doing so could undermine the entire process.

1. Teachers must intentionally teach the classroom routines to the students starting on the first day.

It is crucial to establish expectations right from the start. On the first day, students will naturally seek to determine the standards of behavior for the classroom. If teachers fail to establish clear expectations immediately, students will fill the void by setting their own standards, which often leads to chaos.

Teaching classroom routines should be like teaching academic topics. There should be a mixture of direct instruction, teacher demonstrations, student practice, and assessments to check for student understanding. Teachers who have well-managed classrooms take this process seriously. Each aspect of the teaching process must be intentional.

During the process, teachers must not rush through either aspect. If it is clear students do not understand a particular routine, then it is well worth the time to go back through the steps of reteaching, demonstrating, and practicing. It will be difficult to create and maintain a productive learning environment if students can't master the classroom routines. Therefore, it is imperative to be deliberate and intentional with this step and continue teaching the process for the number of days necessary for mastery.

2. Make sure parents are aware of the classroom routines.

This step is one that is often overlooked. Many teachers feel parents don't want to know the details of how they manage their classroom. Whether parents want to know or not is an opinion that will vary among teachers. However, I believe parents need to know how their child's classroom is managed.

Therefore, teachers should email a copy of the classroom routines to the student's parents. The routines should also be posted on the teachers' webpage if one is available. The classroom routines should be included in the teacher's newsletter to parents. Along with a copy of the routines, teachers should explain their importance.

Teachers should include in their parent communication asking the parents for their support by stressing to their child the importance of following the classroom routines. This will send a message to parents that you want them to be an active partner in their child's education. I provide more details on partnering with parents in Chapter 7. You may be pleasantly surprised by the effectiveness of this step. Try it and see!

3. Randomly test students' knowledge of routines.

Effective educators constantly check for understanding and mastery as they are teaching their content. Classroom routines should be no different. It is very important for teachers to intentionally plan times to check students' knowledge and understanding of the classroom routines.

These assessments can take various forms, such as lighthearted games, written quizzes, verbal questioning, or integrating routine-related questions into bell work or exit slips. Regardless of the method used, the results should be analyzed to identify gaps in understanding. This process reinforces the importance of routines and ensures students internalize expectations.

Regardless of the method teachers use to assess students' understanding, it is important to use the assessment results to make sure students have a working knowledge of the classroom routines. Doing so sends a clear message to students that the classroom routines are important and they are expected to know them and follow them. The teacher's priorities generally become the students' priorities. It's amazing how that works!

4. Celebrate student and class mastery of routines.

This is an important step for several reasons. First, students need to know when they have reached the classroom goals. Once they do, it is important for teachers to express an appreciation of their students' accomplishments. That can be done with some type of celebration. The magnitude of the celebration is up to the teacher. I suggest that it matches the level of difficulty of the routine. The more difficult the routine, the bigger the celebration.

Another reason to celebrate is that it provides students with some positive reinforcement. When teachers make a big deal of students' behavior, it tends to motivate them to continue that behavior. A celebration is a great way to motivate students to continue a specific classroom routine. If there is a certain routine deemed more important than others, then it may be appropriate for teachers to choose that one to celebrate once it is mastered.

Celebrations can also send a message to students that their work and commitment can be personally beneficial to them. Most students I have taught needed to get something tangible for their work. Usually, the tangible benefits were less important once the students got into a habit with the routines. They ended up following classroom routines without even thinking about it. It was a beautiful thing.

5. Revisit classroom routines after two or three weeks.

Once students have had plenty of practice and experience working on classroom routines, it is important to evaluate the routines to see if there are adjustments needed. This is good practice for continuous improvement, which should always be the goal. Most of us want to be as effective as possible. This is a way to help increase effectiveness.

An important part of this step is to allow for student input. Teachers should pose questions to their students to gather input on the effectiveness of the classroom routines. Remember, the teacher initially developed these routines without any student input. So, now that students have engaged in the classroom routines for a period of time, they can provide some valuable insight that can be used to make adjustments.

Ultimately, the teacher retains authority over any adjustments, but this step demonstrates a collaborative approach and fosters student ownership. Often, students' suggestions are minimal, as they have already established a comfort level with the existing routines.

Hopefully, you now have a firm grasp of how to effectively establish expectations in your classroom by developing classroom norms and routines. They are both essential to having a positive and productive learning environment. However, even the most thoughtful educators with well-developed norms and routines will have students who don't follow them. That is when the teacher must implement a consequence. The next section will provide details on implementing consequences when students don't meet the expectations.

Consequences

Implementing consequences is primarily about disciplining students. It is important for me first to share my philosophy on disciplining students. By doing so, I hope this will provide some background knowledge to help you understand the methods I have used in the past. This is all based on my experiences and perspective as an educator, administrator, and researcher.

I am certain that teachers reading this will have diverse reactions to the strategies I outline. Some may entirely disagree, others may completely agree, and some may find themselves in partial agreement with certain strategies while questioning others. Ultimately, each teacher must discern what is most appropriate for their students. That, in many ways, is the beauty of teaching: the ability to adapt and choose what aligns with the unique needs of your students. Let us now explore this topic in depth.

Consequences, or disciplinary actions, are issued when expectations are not met. While expectations revolve around providing clear instructions for desired behaviors, consequences are about addressing deviations from, or violations of, those expectations. My core belief is that consequences should be used to correct inappropriate behavior rather than to inflict harm or act as punishment.

From my experience, effective consequences require an element of accountability that inconveniences or creates a degree of discomfort for students. Without this, the consequence may fail to motivate behavioral change. Importantly, no single disciplinary action universally motivates all students. Each child reacts differently, requiring a nuanced, individualized approach to ensure the consequence is impactful.

My philosophy has always been to implement disciplinary actions on a minimum-to-maximum continuum. The range of disciplinary actions I implemented went from no action to an office referral. As you might guess, no action is on the minimum end of the continuum and office referrals were on the maximum end. I know it may seem hard to understand how no action can be considered a consequence. I will be sure to explain in more detail exactly what I mean with this minimum consequence in the sections to follow. I will also provide details on the maximum end of the continuum and all the steps between.

The guiding principle in issuing consequences is to start with the least invasive measure that is still effective in correcting the behavior. My role as a teacher was to cultivate an environment underpinned by norms that benefited all students. Just as norms must be consistently reinforced to nurture a positive environment, consequences must be applied consistently to preserve it.

As I previously stated, my goal was to start with the least amount of discipline when working with a situation. I also stated earlier that the minimum was to take no action. My version of taking no action was to acknowledge the student's inappropriate behavior and then let the student know that I was choosing to waive my right to issue consequences.

Having clarified this, I will now delve into the range of consequences I utilized in most classroom situations. For each, I will provide a succinct explanation of how it was implemented. My continuum of consequences included:

- Teacher Conferences

- Reflection Time

- Loss of Privileges

- Detention

- Combination of consequences

- Office referral

As you read through my detailed explanation of these consequences, you should ponder how each one might fit into your teaching style and the extent to which your students may or may not respond to each.

Teacher Conferences

Whenever a student engaged in behavior that warranted a consequence, my first step was always to hold a teacher conference. This marked the beginning of the disciplinary process, regardless of whether additional measures were followed. These conferences are critical for reinforcing your position as the authority figure in the classroom and for fostering a mutual understanding of expectations.

The depth and scope of the conference depended on the nature of the infraction. For minor behaviors, such as being off task or engaging in an unauthorized conversation, the conference was brief-a quick, corrective comment redirecting the student toward appropriate behavior.

In a more serious situation, such as causing a major disruption with reckless behavior or a major argument with a classmate, then there would be a more in-depth conversation that included a series of questions. The questions I used in most conferences were as follows:

- What happened?

- Who else was involved?

- What was your role in the situation?

- What did you do to try to avoid being in this situation?

- Did you have any other options? If so, what were they? If not, why not?

- Who was impacted by this situation?

- What needs to happen to correct the situation?

While not every situation required going through all these questions, they provided a useful framework. Sometimes, additional follow-up questions were necessary to clarify the student's perspective or explore specific details further.

After going through these questions, I would then make sure there was a specific plan in place to bring closure to the situation. If the situation required more time to finalize, I would be sure to set up the targeted timeframe for completion and then follow up to make sure everything was completed. If everything went according to the plan then the result was as intended. If not, then I would go through parts of the process again to determine how to best bring closure to the situation.

Teacher conferences proved highly effective because they eliminated ambiguity for the student. By clearly defining the problem and the steps to address it, these conferences set students up for success.

Reflection Time

This consequence was a good one to use with my students. It was used primarily to give students time to think about what happened and consider how they might do things differently in the future. I usually required students to write a brief summary of their reflection to use as a focal point of our discussion of their behavior.

When implementing this consequence, I used a range of time periods. The period was usually between five and 20 minutes. To determine the amount of time assigned, I would consider the severity of the infraction. Minor infractions would result in a short period, while more serious infractions would lead to longer periods. Most often, the maximum I used was about 20 minutes.

When assigning reflection time, I considered the student's personality and behavioral tendencies. For instance, highly social students found isolation more impactful than introverted students, who might not perceive isolation as a consequence. This awareness allowed me to customize reflection periods for maximum effectiveness.

For example, students who are highly social would be impacted more by a reflection period of isolation than students who are introverts. Therefore, a five-minute reflection period may seem like an eternity for the socialite, and that same five-minute period may feel like one minute to the introvert. You have to know your students to make the best decision.

Another consideration would be the number of times I used this option as a consequence. My belief was that there should be a progression over time. I would always try to begin with the least amount of time and increase as needed.

If the violation occurred multiple times for the same type of infraction, then I would progressively increase the reflection time. This process of repeating this consequence was used maybe a maximum of three times. If the behavior continued, then I would move to another type of consequence. I concluded at this point that this was the student's way of showing me this consequence was not working. Remember, the ultimate goal is to see a change in behavior.

I must mention that I would always make an exception to this consequence and allow students to join the class when it was a critical learning situation that could not easily be replicated, such as an academic lab or group activity. I did not want students to feel as though they were totally isolated from the class and begin to lose their self-esteem or sense of belonging.

Loss of Privileges

It is important to note that teachers should incorporate a variety of privileges in their classrooms. This provides some leverage to remove privileges as part of this consequence.

When I was a student, my teachers often reminded me that I had all the privileges I needed when they provided me with an opportunity to get my education. Keep in mind that it is inappropriate and illegal if educational opportunity is the main privilege a teacher takes away from students. Legally, students have a right to an education.

Instead, I worked to establish privileges in other areas. For example, I might allow students certain classroom responsibilities, access to preferred seating, or opportunities to participate in non-academic activities. Removing these privileges as a disciplinary measure proved to be a powerful motivator.

When removal of privileges is used as a consequence, it is essential to start with less impactful measures and then progressively escalate to more significant ones if necessary. Some of the privileges might include listening to music, access to personal devices, sitting in a lounge area, or enjoying free time. This list deliberately excluded occasional activities like assemblies, festivals, or parties, which I reserved as special incentives to handle situations on a case-by-case basis.

When implementing this consequence, I would determine which privilege was most appropriate to take and then how long to take it. Some privileges were allowed daily, and some were granted periodically. My decision often depended on the frequency of the privilege.

I may have taken away a weekly activity privilege for one week, which would mean the student would only miss that opportunity one time. I wasn't so concerned about this as much as I tried to determine what would impact the students enough to change the unwanted behavior. There were other times that I needed to deny the opportunity to attend a major event that the student had spent weeks looking forward to. This created an impact that was much more consequential than some of the routine privileges.

Another critical aspect of removing privileges was ensuring minimal disruption to others. I was careful not to cause collateral inconvenience to myself, other students, or any individuals who depended on the student. For instance, I rarely removed a privilege that would negatively affect their peer group or school teams. I did not want others to suffer because of their mistake. However, I would use the opportunity to point out the potential impact their actions might have had on their team if their participation had been removed. This approach served as a teachable moment, emphasizing how their behavior could affect the people connected to them.

Overall, this consequence proved effective. It is vital to assess which privileges resonate most with your students to achieve the desired behavioral change. Some students might be indifferent to the loss of certain privileges but are deeply affected by losing others. Observing their engagement and enthusiasm during normal circumstances is an excellent way to gauge which privileges hold the most weight.

Once you identify the privilege to remove, it's important to remain firm and consistent in applying the consequence. Following through with the decision sends a clear message that you mean what you say. Interestingly, this often acts as a powerful deterrent, discouraging students from testing boundaries again.

Detentions

When the loss of privileges failed to motivate behavioral change, the next step was to assign detention. This consequence was designed to create a degree of inconvenience, helping students understand that their actions carried tangible repercussions. Importantly, I always strived to make the detention relevant to the student or the specific behavior being addressed.

I utilized several types of detentions: before school, during lunch, or after school. The choice depended on which option would have the most meaningful impact on the student. For instance, some students cherished social interactions during lunch, so assigning them a lunch detention proved particularly effective. Other students eagerly anticipated spending time in their neighborhood after school. After-school detention was more impactful with these students. Conversely, some students welcomed staying after school to avoid going home; for them, after-school detention was ineffective.

Another factor I would consider was to connect the consequence to the behavior. If the student showed inappropriate behavior during lunch, then a lunch detention would likely be the consequence. If the inappropriate behavior happened getting off the bus in the morning, then a before school detention would be the consequence. This helped the student to understand the relevance of the consequence of the behavior.

An additional point to note is that I would issue multiple days of detention if the behavior was more severe. Therefore, the severity of the infraction determined not only the type of detention but also the number of times or days they would have to serve it. For example, if it was because of a physical altercation, then I may issue more than one day of detention.

I need to also point out that I also required the students to engage in more thoughtful reflection of their behavior during the time they served the detention. They had to write a more detailed description of the incident and their plan of action to avoid the inappropriate behavior in the future. This reflective writing was used as the focal point of a more engaging conference with the student. This usually was the main reason students didn't want to experience this consequence again.

The last part of this consequence was the communication with the student's parents. When consequences got to this level, parent communication was part of the process. The consequences before this step may have included parent communication if it happened more than once. However, a detention consequence meant an automatic parent contact the first time. Needless to say, this was a very powerful aspect of this consequence.

Overall, this approach taught students several valuable lessons. They learned that they were accountable for their actions, that their choices could cause inconvenience to themselves, and that thoughtful reflection could lead to better decision-making in the future. It also reinforced the idea that their ability to control their own time was tied directly to their behavior.

A consequence is only effective if it has a genuine adverse impact on the student. The more significant the impact, the more likely the consequence will drive a change in behavior. For most students, this step in the disciplinary process was effective in achieving this goal.

Combination of Consequences

There were occasions when the previous steps alone did not completely take care of the issue. It was at this point that I had to determine the next disciplinary action I needed to implement to see a change in behavior. This was a rare situation because students typically would respond appropriately to the initial consequence that I issued to them.

When I implemented a consequence, I did not expect perfection. However, I did require a noticeable improvement in the student's behavior. Sometimes, a lack of response to the initial consequence necessitated further action. In other cases, the student might repeat an inappropriate behavior that I had already addressed. In the times I had to go down that road, my process was to look at the situation and go back to one or more of the other consequences. Most often, I would use a combination of consequences.

For example, I would use reflection time and loss of privileges as a combination of consequences. There were times I would use the loss of privileges and detention to provide the necessary correction to their behavior. This step in the process served as a way to bring more intensity to the consequence.

The number of times I used a combination of disciplinary actions and the level of intensity depending upon how often the inappropriate behavior occurred. I also considered the seriousness of the behavior.

As I have mentioned before, it was rare that I had to intensify the consequences due to my students not being able to correct their behavior. However, when I did have to move to this step, I tried to be even more intentional about matching the consequence to the behavior. I also was more attentive to the uniqueness of my students when it came to this level of disciplinary action. I will note that this step was also when I initiated a parent conference to discuss the student's situation and solicit additional support.

In other words, it was no longer a normal or general consequence. Any time the behavior got to this level I had to step back to make sure my communication was effective and their level of understanding was where it needed to be. It didn't matter how much I was teaching them the behavior expectations if they weren't learning it. Therefore, I knew I possibly needed to communicate differently so they would learn the lesson from the situation.

After I felt comfortable with my communication and the process I chose to use, then there were no internal guilty feelings or sense of doubt lingering in my head. As I reached that comfort zone, I had more assurance that I was on the right path. The next step for me at this point was to stay with my decision and let the process work out. The overwhelming majority of the time, it worked out. That meant we achieved the desired successful outcome.

Office Referrals

In the most extreme and rare cases, when every other disciplinary action proved ineffective or when the behavior was excessively severe, I resorted to issuing an office referral. I want to emphasize that this was a last resort-a measure I used sparingly.

Admittedly, it was my least preferred option, but it remained a necessary tool in my disciplinary repertoire. Its effectiveness lay in its rarity; my students understood that crossing certain lines would have serious consequences. The mere possibility of an office referral served as a strong deterrent.

So, what constituted an uncrossable line? For me, one clear boundary was engaging in physical altercations or fighting in the classroom. This was an absolute no-go in my classroom. I invested considerable time and energy in helping my students understand the importance of maintaining a peaceful and supportive learning environment.

Many of my students had dysfunctional family units, and they desperately wanted and needed to bond with someone. Fighting would damage that bond, and I was determined not to let that cause them to experience that level of malfunction in their relationships. It worked out quite well because the students managed to coexist without having any physical fights in the classroom.

The other reason an office referral may have been the disciplinary action was if their behavior involved them being deliberately or blatantly disrespectful for an extended period. I would first make sure the students were intentionally behaving in this manner before I would resort to an office referral.

To further explain, sometimes a student would be extremely upset and became disrespectful. The behavior may have been general in nature as opposed to directed at a peer or me. If the student continued the behavior for an extended time period after I intervened, then I would let them know the next step would be an office referral.

Even then, I did not always issue an office referral. It depended on the frequency and intensity. As a teacher, you will know the type of relationship you have with your students and when to take the consequence to the next level. This type of behavior usually did not result in an office referral the first time. However, I didn't allow this behavior to happen many times before I quickly took serious action.

I was very clear in my communication with students prior to the possibility of an office referral being an option. I had a proven history of following through with what I told them, and that helped them to know what the discipline options would be as they moved toward an office referral becoming a consequence. I believe that was very helpful to them by eliminating any surprises and allowing them to make more conscious decisions. In my opinion, that was the fair way to do it.

Speaking of being fair, I think it is important for me to point out that I tried to be fair when I used office referrals as the disciplinary action. I felt there were some factors that needed to be considered to ensure the use of this consequence in a fair and reasonable manner. The bulleted points below include my thoughts prior to deciding to issue an office referral:

- Make sure to communicate to students that this will be an option prior to deciding to do it.

- Be sure it is within the guidelines of building policies.

- Be sure not to be angry when writing an office referral.

- Be sure that this is best for the student.

- Be sure it is a last resort. That means no other option is likely to work or has worked.

When I was convinced that these points were adequately addressed then I was okay with making the decision to use this consequence. When I decided this was the appropriate consequence, I contacted the parent to arrange for an in-person conference. The conversation was always to inform the parent as well as get the parents' support to help change the student's behavior. It was also to get the parents, student, and me on the same page with the expectations moving forward. Most often, the parents appreciated the conference and expressed their support. I believe it was mainly because they knew it had to be something very serious since I asked them to sit for an in-person conference.

My rare use of this consequence also had an impact on students. Therefore, just the mentioning of a potential office referral helped eliminate the thought of them engaging in inappropriate behaviors that were serious enough for this consequence. I did not mention it unless I was serious about the possibility of doing it. My students knew if I said it, I meant it. The good news is that I didn't have to mention office referrals or issue them much at all. I call that a success!

This concludes the steps in my disciplinary process. I have noticed during my career that some teachers may not get the results they want because they aren't consistent. There are times when teachers don't implement the consequences for a long enough period. Another reason for poor results could be because of feelings of guilt. Teachers can fall into the trap of guilt by thinking they are doing something "to" the students. You must realize that you are doing something "for" the students. Taking disciplinary action is primarily for the purpose of minimizing or eliminating the inappropriate behaviors that might cause students not to get the most out of their educational experience.

Be reminded that it is extremely important to be very clear with your students about what is expected and the consequences of not meeting those expectations. Students do much better when they know what to expect from their teachers. In addition, you should remember the importance of saying what you mean and meaning what you say. Following through is of the utmost importance. This alone can make or break the entire process of setting expectations and implementing consequences.

Also, never underestimate the power of positive reinforcement. Acknowledging and celebrating your students' successes, no matter how small, can transform their self-confidence and motivation. A balanced approach that combines clear expectations, fair consequences, and genuine encouragement can lead to extraordinary results.

Throughout this chapter, there is information on setting the expectations and consequences. This information is not meant to be all-inclusive as it relates to expectations and consequences. I can attest that it was not effective for all situations and all students. I have merely shared the major points that I feel will provide the most insight into the overall success I experienced.

If you feel you have followed the strategies with fidelity but still did not get the desired results, you may want to consider getting more professional support. This might include professional development, mentoring, or administrator support. To determine which direction to take, it would be best to engage in some meaningful reflection. Chapter 3 provides more details on a reflection process.

In the next chapter, I will shift focus to instructional strategies. While many of these concepts may be familiar to you, they will serve as a valuable refresher-or an opportunity to learn new techniques that can elevate your teaching practice.

Chapter 5

⬩⬩⬩❧⬩⬩⬩

INSTRUCTIONAL FOCUS

You are probably aware that there are countless educators, presenters, and researchers offering an extensive array of suggestions regarding the factors that contribute to quality instruction. Similarly, many experts have pointed out what teachers should avoid doing when striving to deliver effective instruction. Both perspectives provide valuable insights that can help teachers refine their practices and improve student outcomes.

In this chapter, I will first explore six key areas where I believe teachers should concentrate their instructional focus. As with other lists I have shared, this is not intended to be an exhaustive collection of strategies. Rather, the areas I discuss represent some of the most critical dimensions I consider essential for teachers aiming to deliver high-quality instruction.

The second part of the chapter concludes with a concise discussion of ten areas that can present significant challenges for teachers, particularly if they make suboptimal decisions in those domains. The information in this chapter reflects my interpretation of educational literature and research on effective instruction, as well as lessons I've gleaned from my personal experiences as an educator and administrator in evaluating and implementing instructional practices.

Six Key Areas

I believe there are six key areas to explore as teachers attempt to focus on instruction are included in the following list of items.

- Teachers' beliefs

- Students' current knowledge

- Information students need to know

- Help students learn

- Process to determine students' knowledge

- Next steps

Richard Dufour's professional learning communities (PLC) model mainly influences these focus areas. Dufour uses four critical questions for teachers to discuss so that learning can be personalized for students.

With Dufour's work as the foundation, I have added two additional points that can help teachers better grasp how to approach this area. The ultimate goal is to increase the likelihood of instructional effectiveness. So, let me go deeper into the six points shared above.

1. Teachers' Beliefs

This is an exceptionally important point. Teachers' beliefs ultimately shape how they prepare for lessons. Their preparation, in turn, influences their actions in the classroom, which affects how students respond. This chain of influence ultimately determines the effectiveness of instruction. For this reason, teachers' belief systems should be anchored in four fundamental principles when focusing on instruction.

First, teachers must believe that all students are capable of learning. If a teacher believes that a student cannot learn, the likelihood of achieving a meaning result diminishes significantly. Teachers' expectations often become self-fulfilling prophecies: expecting success usually yields success. Admittedly, exceptions exist-for instance, students with medically diagnosed cognitive disabilities who require specialized support tailored to their unique circumstances. However, teachers must begin with this foundational belief for all other students.

A second core belief teachers must hold is that all students can be motivated. Students can be motivated to learn in different ways. Some of them come with a natural curiosity to learn, whereas others need to be encouraged. Teachers must believe that all students will be motivated if they use the correct techniques. This belief should encourage teachers to constantly strive to figure out what drives their students.

The third belief is that teachers are responsible for their students' learning. Parents entrust their children's education to schools, and the classroom teacher shoulders the primary responsibility for ensuring that learning takes place. This responsibility does not rest with support staff, media specialists, or administrators-it rests with the teacher. Without this core belief, it becomes easy for educators to rationalize underperformance by blaming external factors. Teachers must embrace this accountability during lesson planning, collaboration, and the development of instructional activities.

The fourth core belief is that teachers must believe their efforts will make a difference. This is generally referred to as teacher efficacy. Teachers get discouraged because they don't always see the impact of their efforts. I have seen far too many examples of the exceptional impact of a teacher on students four or five years later. Therefore, teachers must take comfort that as they consistently use sound professional practice, the results will follow either when they have the students or at some point in the future. Teachers do make a difference!

Teachers need to hold these four core beliefs to have an approach to instruction that will yield the best results for students. It may take additional evidence for some teachers to agree with this completely, but I encourage all teachers to evaluate their mindset to determine exactly where they fall. If you are struggling with one or more of these beliefs, you might want to have some discussions with some trusted colleagues or your administrator.

2. Students' Current Knowledge

Understanding students' current knowledge is the essential first step in instruction. Teachers must establish a baseline before introducing new material. Unfortunately, many educators begin teaching without adequately assessing what their students already know, a misstep that can lead to ineffective instruction or even harm students academically and emotionally.

First, teachers should avoid making assumptions about what students know. Just because the students took a prerequisite class, it doesn't mean they learned all the material from that class. The same holds true from one grade level to the next grade level. If you make assumptions about students' current knowledge, it will cause you to miss the mark and there is a chance you will cause greater academic harm and possibly even emotional harm to the students.

Therefore, teachers should take specific steps to determine exactly where students are in their knowledge. This means teachers will have to be attentive to the individuality of their students. To get to the learning levels of the students, teachers will need to give assessments that will capture the correct information. Assessments that are too lengthy will either include too many concepts or too many items on the same concept. Therefore, be succinct with your assessments to capture exactly what you need to know.

The next important point to consider when determining what students know is more about the methods teachers use to assess students. It is important not to let this type of assessment lead to inaccurate results. Teachers are professionals, and it is important for teachers to go into their professional toolkit to find the right type of assessment for each student. Most students respond well to paper and pencil assessments. Some students may need a verbal assessment. Others may need to show their level of understanding using manipulatives or some type of demonstration. It is up to the teacher to recognize which assessment method works best and be confident enough to believe it reflects students' current knowledge.

3. Information Students Need To Know

Once students' current knowledge has been assessed, the focus shifts to the material they need to learn. This step can be challenging if teachers lack a clear framework or become sidetracked. To avoid potential pitfalls, consider the following points as general guidelines.

The first point is that teachers must be familiar with the required curriculum they need to teach. This helps to keep from getting off track by spending too much time on concepts that are on the periphery of the main learning targets. This happens more than we care to admit. Time is valuable and it is important for teachers to stay focused on the learning requirements so that students get the most benefit out of the instruction.

The next point is that teachers need to make sure to teach the new material at the appropriate level. There must be consideration given to the degree of difficulty as well as age appropriateness. This is important when having discussions or using examples during lessons. Students may struggle to learn new material that is over their heads if they haven't been provided enough background knowledge. Caution must be taken to avoid them getting distracted because of inappropriate material for their age. That can include both ends of the spectrum with materials that can be too mature or too immature for the students. Teachers should avoid letting this hinder what students need to know.

A final point I want to make is that teachers need to stress to students the benefits of learning the material. Teachers should be able to tell students why they need to know the material. Students want to know that the material is relevant to their lives. Therefore, teachers should be sure to have some real-life examples of how the material can be applied in the real world. It will make a tremendous difference to the students. I believe this will increase the effectiveness of the instruction.

4. Help Students Learn

Now that it has been determined what students need to know, we can proceed to explore strategies to help them acquire the new material. Teachers must carefully consider the most effective ways to engage students in learning the required concepts. By now, it should be evident that teachers' actions significantly impact student outcomes. Therefore, teachers must evaluate several factors when identifying the best approach to maximize student learning.

The first factor teachers should consider is engaging in purposeful and strategic lesson planning. I believe the basic structure of a teacher's lesson plan can substantially increase the likelihood of students mastering the material. An effective structure I have found consists of at least four key parts. First, the lesson should include an introductory phase, which can be facilitated through direct instruction or student discovery. Next, teacher modeling should follow, clearly demonstrating the concept or skill. The third step involves guided practice, where the teacher collaborates with students to reinforce understanding. Finally, students should be able to work independently to demonstrate their grasp of the material. This allows the teacher to check for understanding. These four components do not always have to follow a strict sequence but should be present in some capacity within every lesson format.

The second factor to consider is for teachers to comprehensively understand their students' learning styles. This knowledge will assist teachers during the lesson-planning phase. Recognizing the diversity in learning preferences enables teachers to be more thoughtful and intentional while designing their lessons. This awareness allows educators to incorporate activities that cater to kinesthetic, auditory, or visual learners. There is extensive research on these learning styles, and I strongly recommend that teachers familiarize themselves with this literature to support their students better.

The last factor to consider is determining the type of activities to include in the lesson plan. This is mainly about teachers knowing the personality of the classroom. Not all activities are created equally. What works for one class may not work the same for another class. Therefore, teachers need to design unique activities for the classroom personality. I understand that it is much easier to develop one set of lesson plans for all classes of the same subject. However, that is not always what is best for the students. For example, the dynamics in one class may prohibit any form of group work, but another class may function better with group work. Teachers must be able to determine the best approach to increase the learning opportunities for the students.

5. Process to Determine Students' Knowledge

This step in the instructional focus process is arguably the most critical for guiding teachers' efforts. At this stage, educators must develop meaningful ways to gather data on students' levels of understanding. Let's explore a few considerations.

One primary method of monitoring students' knowledge is through the use of assessments. As mentioned earlier, assessments should be designed to evaluate what students know about a given topic. These assessments should be ongoing, a practice referred to as formative assessment. At some point, students will take a final assessment, known as a summative assessment. Both formative and summative assessments provide teachers with valuable data to inform instruction.

Another important consideration when evaluating students' knowledge is determining the frequency of assessments. I believe teachers should assess students daily. Remember that assessments should serve as a guide for instruction. Therefore, if teachers collect assessment data daily, they can adjust their instructional strategies accordingly. It is important to note that assessments do not always have to be a written quiz or test. Alternatives such as exit slips, bell work at the start of class, or individual and group questioning can also yield valuable data for teachers to guide their focus.

The last consideration I want to share is that teachers must incorporate a process requiring students to obtain the knowledge. Teachers should not allow students to opt out of learning. This is mainly about teachers establishing the expectations of students' effort to learn. Students will live up to or down to the level teachers expect of them. It is very important for teachers to consistently hold high expectations that students put forth an effort to learn. That also means that teachers must continuously monitor or assess students' level of effort. It will make a significant difference in the learning results.

6. Next Steps

Teachers need to have a clear and actionable plan once they determine whether or not students have achieved the desired learning outcomes. As one might expect, the results will likely vary, with some students mastering the material and others requiring additional support.

After analyzing the assessment data, teachers must determine how to address the needs of students who have not mastered the material. These students will need further exposure to the content through strategically planned reteaching efforts. Educators must establish the most appropriate methods for reteaching, identify the necessary time commitment, and decide when the reteaching will occur. While there are multiple ways to approach this process, the key is to ensure it is intentional and systematically implemented. Simply being aware of gaps in students' understanding is insufficient; teachers must actively work to close those gaps.

On the other side of the coin for teachers is determining what to do with the students who learned the material. There needs to be meaningful enrichment opportunities for students when they have mastered the material. If this is the majority of the students, then the instruction was quite effective, and it may be time to move on to the next concept. If it is a small group of students, it may be an opportunity for the students to engage in an extension activity. It could also allow the students to become peer coaches and reteach the material to their classmates. Whatever the strategy, it is important for teachers to have a plan to engage this group of students.

After teachers have addressed the needs of both groups of students, they should carve out some time to reflect on the instructional focus process. The reflection should include the steps outlined in the Reflection section of Chapter 3. It is up to the teacher to truthfully examine all the steps that were taken during the process and make corrections to improve future performance. It is necessary to consider the nuances of each student and class of students when examining situations. A variety of factors will be revealed that will surely get you out of your comfort zone if you are truly honest with yourself. However, this disruption is what will help you get better results from your instruction.

This concludes the discussion of the six key areas teachers should consider when focusing on instruction. In the next section of this chapter, I will share my insights on 10 general concepts that educators encounter daily. While these concepts can be controversial, they are unavoidable and merit thoughtful consideration.

General Concepts

Teaching is not an easy profession, and classroom instruction, in particular, is difficult to master. In addition to the six key areas discussed, even the most experienced educators wrestle with numerous other factors that directly and indirectly influence their teaching practices. In this section, I have identified 10 general concepts that I believe are important for teachers to reflect on and form a position regarding. I will also share my stance on each concept and encourage you to engage in further research to solidify your perspective. You may refer to the Additional Resources section after Chapter 7 to get you started.

1. Assessment Retakes

Assessments are necessary to determine the level of knowledge students possess. Teachers must assess students in some manner to inform the next steps in their instruction. Many teachers get stuck in the traditional mindset that an assessment must be on a specific date for all the students at the same time. That may be an acceptable practice. However, there will be times when students don't do well and need more practice or guidance on a concept.

At this point, teachers must decide whether to allow students to have an additional opportunity to show mastery of the assessment. I believe that students should be given multiple opportunities to show mastery. There are very few things students will encounter in the real world that will not allow for additional opportunities to "get it right" with another attempt. We often subscribe to self-imposed deadlines that create more stress for teachers and students.

2. Zero As A Grade

Grades are designed to communicate what students know about a given concept or subject. This may be one of the most controversial topics in education. Once again, many teachers get stuck in tradition and don't take the time to really examine what they are communicating and how they do so when assigning grades. For the most part, the field of education continues to operate on the A-to-F grading continuum. Whether that is appropriate is an argument for another time.

Given this generally accepted grading continuum, there needs to be more thoughtful discussion about how zeros impact a student's grade. In my view, a zero should not be assigned. A zero communicates that the student knows nothing about the concept or topic. I find that to be highly unlikely. Instead of a zero, I suggest the teacher record the assignment or assessment as incomplete until further assessments have been taken. This approach will often lead to more effort by the students and higher grades. Alternatively, it might also be effective to break up the assignment and add the scores together for a better overall grade.

3. Student Technology Use During Instruction

Technology has become a fundamental tool in today's classrooms. It is even more prevalent with individual students since many of them own electronic devices or as schools issue devices to students. As a result, in a large number of classrooms, technology is in the hands of students every day. This means that teachers must manage student technology whether they want to or not.

I believe that teachers will be smart to embrace the technology and intentionally incorporate ways to use it in their lesson plans. This should include personal cell phones that students have or school-issued devices. However, I will caution teachers to make sure the access is equitable. By this, I mean that all students should have access to technology, school-issued or personal devices, if that is part of the activity in the lesson. Teachers must also have clear routines for using the technology appropriately.

4. Homework Policy

Homework, by definition, means work done at home. Many people agree with this definition, but others have taken a much broader position. Some categorize homework as any work that students do outside of the regular classroom lesson, whether at home or school. This includes work completed at the end of a class period or after school in an individual or group setting somewhere in the building.

Rather than focus on where it is done, I will mainly discuss why it should be done. I believe homework should be assigned either to introduce students to a concept that is coming up or as additional practice on a concept already covered. In either case, a teacher's homework policy should not be to assign a grade on the homework. One of the main reasons is that there is no concrete evidence that the student is the one who completed the assignment. Additionally, if the homework introduces a new topic, then it is not appropriate to grade students on material that has not been previously taught by the teacher.

5. Differentiated Instruction

Differentiated instruction (DI) is another topic that has been widely debated among educators for many years. The core premise of this concept is for teachers to design instruction that accounts for the individual learning needs of the students they are teaching.

Although DI is challenging, it is not as difficult as people often assume. I suggest that if teachers consistently assess their students, it is easier to determine what each student needs. The most difficult part is that many teachers aren't willing to adapt and make the necessary adjustments to their instruction. Consider this analogy: What if doctors treated all types of illnesses the same way-using the same medicine, surgical procedures, and rehabilitation plans? You would expect the doctor to differentiate their approach because it could be a matter of life or death. Teachers should be just as serious about differentiating their instruction.

6. Special Education

Teachers must consider the needs of students with special needs. There are specific challenges associated with special education, and those challenges require educators to rely heavily on teachers who specialize in that area. Most academic programs require all educators to take one or two courses geared toward understanding students with special needs. However, this requirement barely scratches the surface of the knowledge that teachers need.

To better equip educators, I believe it is essential for regular education and special education teachers who share the same students to collaborate often. This will allow time for teachers to review students' individualized education programs (IEPs) continuously. Too often, special education teachers send out initial IEPs or review them with teachers at the start of the school year and never discuss them again. This approach is not acceptable. There must be an intentional effort to stay current on the needs of each student.

7. Culturally Relevant Teaching

Culturally relevant teaching has become more and more controversial with recent changes in the political climate. There is an effort by some politicians to avoid any discussion of the different cultures in schools. Many people try to limit cultural discussion to that of race or ethnic groups. The truth is a common culture connects many individuals. Students can connect to others culturally by neighborhoods, churches, gender, or athletics to name a few.

With this in mind, I suggest that teachers make a special point to include culturally relevant examples, pictures, and activities in their lesson plans. Students tend to be more attentive and interested when they have a personal connection. That means teachers must take the time to learn about the cultures represented in their classrooms. Culturally relevant teaching, when done appropriately, can be very effective.

8. Extra Credit Work

Extra credit work is the work teachers allow students to do for additional points on their grades. It is usually work that is an extension of the work that the teacher has already assigned. Most teachers use this to help students whose grades are not at the level they want or need to be. This is another traditional concept that is common in schools across the country.

I am not a proponent of extra credit work for grade improvement. I believe that students can do additional work to increase their grades, but I don't think extra credit is appropriate. It should be additional work to make up for the deficiencies in the student's learning, which would get them to where they need to be. This work should be graded normally as part of the required curriculum. If students do extra work beyond the required curriculum, it should be based on an accelerated model covering future material.

9. Late Assignments

This is another commonly debated topic by educators. For various reasons, students sometimes do not turn their assignments in by the deadline teachers set. Teachers then will have to determine how to handle late assignments. To have consistency, teachers need to develop policies on accepting late assignments. Late assignment policies can vary widely among teachers, but the primary concern is usually the impact it might have on a student's grade.

I take a conditional approach to handling late assignments. Basically, it depends on whether the assignment is in-class or out-of-class. If it is an in-class assignment and I can verify the student completed it, I would accept it without penalty. For out-of-class work, late submissions are accepted but not for a grade. Instead, I would issue an alternate assignment covering the same material, which the student can complete in class for full credit. As you can tell, I do not like deducting points from a student's grade for late assignments. If the concept was part of the required curriculum, I want students to learn it during the school year, no matter when it is submitted. Ultimately, it's about ensuring they master the material.

10. Standardized Testing

Standardized tests are a major factor in most school districts. Each state typically uses some form of testing to hold schools accountable for student learning. In most cases these tests are given toward the end of the school year to determine if students are performing on grade level. These tests often cause teachers to experience high levels of stress, which in turn trickles down to the students.

Teachers often fear that they will lose their jobs if students don't perform well. Therefore, many teachers plan standardized test preparation days in hopes of increasing student performance. I don't particularly agree with this approach. Instead, I believe teachers should incorporate into their daily lessons the type of questions students will encounter on standardized tests. This should minimize the stress on both teachers and students. If the teachers have been consistent in their daily teaching, then the students will perform better on the standardized tests.

Hopefully, the information shared in this chapter will help you have a better working knowledge of the important areas and topics to focus on during instruction. Based on my experience and research, focusing on the six key areas and the 10 additional topics will put teachers in a much better position to be effective. Other areas and topics can easily be added, but I am confident that these will provide a firm foundation to any teacher who adopts the positions I suggest.

In the next chapter, I discuss ways teachers should establish support networks. Teachers need to know that they don't have to do this work alone. I hope you find the information beneficial. I certainly have.

Chapter 6

Establish Support Networks

Both teachers and students need plenty of support as they go through their respective educational journeys. One might think it is only the students who need support, but I would argue that teachers need it just as much as their students, if not more.

As you attempt to fulfill your role as the classroom teacher, there are many forces pulling against you. You will sometimes need reassurance along the way to help you stay motivated and to validate that you are going in the right direction. Therefore, it is important for you to establish support networks that help both you and your students. This chapter is designed to encourage all teachers to tap into some resources that will accomplish that goal.

I have met too many teachers who place an excessive amount of the burden of educating students solely upon themselves. Let me share something with you: You cannot shoulder the responsibilities and burdens of teaching alone. It is much bigger than you!

Once you come to terms with this reality, you will be in a much better state of mind. I guarantee that it will relieve a lot of pressure and make you less critical of yourself. You must give yourself permission to make mistakes and come to the realization that you do not, and cannot, know it all.

Once you have achieved the right mindset, you will be much more likely to seek supportive networks to assist you with your students. In the following sections, I will provide guidance on important networks, which I categorize as those that are directly for teachers and those that directly support students. There is some overlap in both categories, wherein the support can be provided directly to both teachers and students.

Teacher-Focused Support

Anyone who decides to become a teacher will need a tremendous amount of support. People in our society are now more critical of teachers than ever before. So, it is very important that teachers have support networks around them to help with the daunting tasks they encounter every day. I believe a few people and groups can play a major role in supporting our teachers.

The list that I share in this section consists of resources that typically have a more direct impact on teachers rather than students. This is not intended to be an all-inclusive list, but it aims to provide some vital resources that all teachers can utilize. As you review the items I share, you may think of some additional resources to include. If so, then you will be an even better educator since there is no such thing as having too much support. The items listed are not in priority order because each has its own unique value. Here we go!

1. Mentors

Mentors are typically assigned to guide new teachers as they begin their careers. However, I believe all teachers who want to grow in the profession can benefit from a mentor. Assuming the teacher's willingness to grow and be mentored, this benefit is most impactful if the mentor is qualified and takes the role seriously.

A qualified mentor is someone who displays the CHEER qualities I have listed in Chapter 2. Qualified mentors should be committed, honest, empathetic, educated, and reflective. They should have enough years of experience such that the advice comes from a thorough knowledge of handling various situations. They also need to have a range of options to be effective in classroom management and instruction.

Another point to consider when identifying mentors is finding someone willing to fulfill the role with genuine dedication. Many times, people accept a mentor role for the extra pay, time off, or a lighter teaching load. Although these benefits are helpful to entice mentors to accept the role, they cannot be the primary reasons for becoming a mentor. Mentors who take the role seriously will spend time with their mentees, hold them accountable, model the way, and provide ongoing, genuine, constructive, and positive feedback.

It is important for both the mentor and the teacher being mentored to be completely invested in the process. There are times when this is not the case. If the mentor-mentee relationship is not working, both parties must acknowledge it and take action for improvement. That may require a new mentor or a change in attitude by the teacher, mentor, or both. Once the aspects I have mentioned are working as intended, the support of a mentor will benefit a teacher beyond measure!

2. Administrators

School administrators play a crucial role in the development of teachers. Administrators are usually the ones who regularly analyze teachers' strengths and challenges. This information can serve as the roadmap for support. A major part of receiving the necessary support is having someone who understands what you truly need. Administrators are in the best position to obtain that knowledge.

Effective administrators support teachers in all the key areas of their roles. They provide professional development opportunities when necessary and know when to scale back on new initiatives to prevent teachers from feeling overwhelmed. As the person with the most knowledge of the total workload, an administrator can also determine which initiatives work best for you and then give you an opportunity to become the expert in that area.

When teachers are referred to as experts on a topic, it enhances their confidence and helps them feel like a valued member of the staff. To further build confidence and foster growth, administrators play an important role in providing constructive classroom observation feedback. Good administrators will highlight the positive attributes they observe in you and share that information with others, instilling confidence that you are progressing.

On the other hand, administrators can also help you grow by providing feedback on areas for growth in both academic and nonacademic areas. Not only will the administrator need to identify growth areas, but also assist with an improvement plan. This can help develop a more targeted plan of support. It is a great way to differentiate the learning. The support will feel much more helpful if it meets a specific need.

These are a few ways that teachers benefit from the support of an administrator. As the teacher who needs this support, you will need to communicate with your administrator about the type of support you need and desire. While independence is vital, you also need and deserve ongoing assistance from your administrator. If you find yourself working under an administrator who is unwilling or unable to provide the support you need, it may be worth reconsidering whether you are in the right environment.

3. Colleagues

Teachers can gain immense support from colleagues. Based on the organizational structure where you teach, the support from colleagues might be by subject, grade level, team, or a combination of these. Regardless of the setup, I suggest that you take full advantage of the support available from your colleagues.

Most schools have time designated for collaboration among teachers. This helps teachers to share ideas on effective ways to perform their duties. Therefore, you will have an opportunity to benefit from the collective knowledge base of those who have found successful strategies in all the tasks associated with teaching. You don't have to reinvent the wheel. Use the resources and support you have around you. It can relieve a lot of stress.

Within any group of colleagues, you will likely find someone who has mastered classroom management, grading practices, parent communication, or other vital aspects of teaching. It is important to be assertive enough to seek the support you need from your colleagues. More often than not, they are willing to help, as it allows them to share their expertise and builds their confidence. Go figure!

A precautionary measure I should mention is that you must also understand that there may be a few instances where the colleague "thinks" the advice being shared is effective, but it may not be sound professional practice. It is up to you to make sure you don't let anyone compromise your professionalism. Therefore, support from colleagues has to be accepted with a critical eye. Your foundation as a teacher has to be built with professionalism at the core. With that in mind, I am sure there are plenty of colleagues who can offer valuable support. It's up to you to get it.

4. Professional Organizations

Becoming a member of a professional organization can significantly expand your support network. These associations cater to a wide range of interests and specialties-whether subject-specific, grade-level oriented, regionally focused, or addressing broader areas of the profession.

Professional organizations often offer a wealth of resources, including workshops, certification courses, and conferences designed to enhance teaching practices. By identifying an organization that aligns with your interests, you can access invaluable opportunities for growth. Attending a conference, for example, allows you to connect with like-minded educators, share experiences, and potentially find mentors who can guide your professional journey.

Professional organizations can be what you make of them. If you don't put much effort into networking with other members or seeking professional development opportunities, you will not get much out of them. Therefore, the results largely depend on your investment. Since many professional organizations focus on so many areas, I won't name a specific organization. However, I will say that I know they can be a valuable support network to anyone who maximizes the use of the benefits they offer.

5. Social Media

Social media platforms have revolutionized the way educators connect and share ideas, offering cost-effective and dynamic forums for professional interaction. Teachers now turn to platforms like Twitter, LinkedIn, and Facebook to exchange advice, showcase successful strategies, and seek input on challenges. This modern avenue of networking provides an ever-expanding reservoir of ideas and resources.

As people share on social media, it is important to thoroughly examine the content being shared to ensure it does not violate your professional code of ethics. Social media is not monitored for accuracy or validity so it is up to each educator to vet the information before adopting it completely. It is also a good way to share ideas and get feedback from other educators in the process. You must be prepared to accept whatever feedback you get, good or bad.

Despite its many advantages, social media presents certain risks. Missteps in its use have led some educators into ethical dilemmas, and in extreme cases, even job loss. Therefore, always adhere to your professional code of ethics and clearly distinguish between your personal and professional online presence. When used thoughtfully and responsibly, social media can be a transformative tool for professional growth, fostering connections that enrich your teaching.

Student-Focused Support

Teachers must establish support networks to help get themselves prepared to work with their students. They also need to look to others for support. There are some key people, groups, and organizations who can provide direct support to students, which in turn supports teachers. With all the challenges teachers face, having as much support as possible is important.

Below, I share some thoughts on a few key people and groups who can provide meaningful support to students. These suggestions are based on my experiences and are intended to inspire you to identify additional resources in your school district or community.

1. Guidance Counselors

Guidance counselors are invaluable for supporting students' academic, social, and emotional development. They collaborate with students to create actionable plans that address challenges, whether academic struggles, behavioral issues, or personal conflicts.

Additionally, guidance counselors play a vital role in fostering classroom harmony. Addressing peer conflicts or teaching students character traits that promote positive interactions help create an environment conducive to learning. Engaged counselors can be transformative, enabling students to overcome obstacles that might otherwise hinder their academic progress.

Teachers should cultivate strong communication with guidance counselors to fully leverage their expertise. Regular dialogue ensures that both parties are aligned in their efforts to support students, ultimately benefiting everyone involved.

2. School Nurses

School nurses work with students constantly during the school day. They must have an extreme amount of patience to be effective. The school nurse is a valuable support for students as they deal with illnesses or injuries. The school nurse can help students get back into the mindset of learning during times when they may not want to. Effective school nurses will rely on their medical training and knowledge of the students to drive their decisions.

Teachers can work closely with school nurses to stay informed about students requiring additional health-related accommodations. Beyond medical care, nurses can also educate students on hygiene and illness prevention, minimizing classroom disruptions caused by avoidable illnesses. A collaborative relationship with the school nurse enhances not only students' well-being but also the overall learning environment.

3. Teacher Colleagues

Teachers should be able to rely on other colleagues to support students. After all, the goal of all teachers should be to help students succeed in their academic journey. This should be the case regardless of the subject or specific content. Most teachers are very passionate about their content and want students to share in their passion. Therefore, they have a personal interest in investing their energy into ensuring student success.

It is important for teachers to rely on each other to support students. That also means teachers must share relevant information so that common strategies are being implemented. The more seamless the message students receive from their teachers, the more effective the message will be. This will ultimately lead to better results for both teachers and students.

The level and scope of support among teacher colleagues can significantly affect how effective a teacher is with students. It is just that important. I suggest that teachers prioritize having thoughtful and intentional conversations with each other regarding the best way to support a shared group of students. I promise there will be a noticeable difference.

4. Media Specialists

Media specialists usually work with students across an entire school building. In essence, they are classroom teachers without a specifically assigned group of students. Media specialists have the difficult task of working with students across different grade levels without all the background information provided to the classroom teachers.

Therefore, teachers should collaborate with media specialists to discuss ways to maximize their support. Teachers can share different tendencies that have been discovered so that the media specialist can be prepared before students arrive. There may be student personality clashes or learning strategies known to work best that would be helpful for the media specialist to know.

Overall, the student support a media specialist can provide mostly depends on your engagement level as the student's teacher. I look at it like dropping your children off to the babysitter without providing the babysitter with any detailed information on your children. The babysitter would be put at a significant disadvantage; thus, your children would not get the best support from the babysitter. So, be engaged and collaborative; you will likely receive maximum student support from your media specialist!

5. Coaches/Club Sponsor

Athletic coaches and club sponsors support students outside the regular classroom. These people play a very important role in supporting students. Many students are invested in school solely because of athletics or clubs. That gives coaches and club sponsors much more influence as they work with students.

Although coaches and club sponsors support students primarily in nonacademic ways, they are still a very important part of the student's school experience. Many times their support can be leveraged in a way to influence students' efforts in their academics. That is why teachers should collaborate with coaches and club sponsors to gain support for their students.

Since many schools and school districts vary on the minimum academic requirements for participation in athletics or clubs, it is up to teachers, coaches and club sponsors to have the moral fortitude to set the academic expectations that best support student success. Once again, it will take continuous collaboration to maximize student support. Teachers should not underestimate the level of support coaches and club sponsors can provide. Give it a try and watch the results. You will be pleasantly surprised.

Throughout this chapter, I have highlighted the importance of establishing robust support networks for both teachers and students. These networks, built on collaboration and mutual respect, are essential for fostering academic achievement and personal growth.

This chapter's teacher-focused and student-focused support networks are primarily located within the school. However, if teachers and schools want to take students to the next level, they must move beyond the school building and get support from outside the building. In the next chapter, I will share information on developing an effective partnership between teachers, parents, and community organizations.

Chapter 7

SCHOOL-HOME-COMMUNITY PARTNERSHIP

In this chapter, I offer suggestions on how teachers in schools can partner with parents and community groups to enhance the likelihood of successful outcomes for students. It is absolutely critical that teachers develop a strong connection with parents. It is also important to leverage community groups to create robust partnerships for the benefit of all students. The reality is that students spend more hours outside of the school setting than they do inside the school. Therefore, it is important that teachers remain aware of what is happening outside of the school environment.

There are a few important areas to focus on to develop a highly effective school-home-community partnership. The most direct interaction within this partnership occurs between teachers and parents. Community groups play a supplementary but valuable role, nonetheless.

Therefore, I will begin with the direct interactions that are necessary between teachers and parents and then end with community groups that can provide valuable assistance in the school-home-community partnership. Attention should be given to both direct parent interactions and indirect community group interactions to maximize the effectiveness of the partnership.

The direct interactions with parents in the partnership can be strengthened by focusing on two important areas: communication and participation. These areas are foundational; however, the extent to which teachers can master each will ultimately determine the partnership's success. Let's look at how to maximize your effectiveness in these areas.

Communication

This is probably the most difficult area to master. In any successful relationship, communication is often the one area that can cause the most difficulty. As you work with students, you will encounter quite a few parents. Consequently, you will need to adapt to a wide range of personalities. It will be to your advantage to get to know your students' parents. The methods you use to communicate, as well as the substance of your communication, are critically important.

To address the methods, I will share the various types of communication that I believe will yield the most effective results. To help you better understand the substance or content of your communication, I will provide insights to guide your conversations.

Methods of Communication

The chosen method of communication can make all the difference in whether your communication is effective. Below, I list several methods in order of effectiveness, starting with what I believe to be the most impactful and ending with the least.

The primary goal is to engage in a dialogue that will help you establish an effective partnership that supports students. Notably, I omitted parents from the support network in the previous chapter to emphasize their critical role in this chapter. So let's go ahead and look at the communication methods.

In-person: This method of communicating is my preferred option. You can have real-time dialogue and get to know your students' parents best using this method. You can do this either by scheduling an individual conference or meeting during scheduled parent-teacher conference days. It is important to know how the parents think, what their philosophy of education is, and how they perceive their child's ability to be a successful student.

When you engage in in-depth conversations, it allows you to listen attentively and ask follow-up questions for clarification. Your goal is to determine the role the parent is going to play in the partnership. While including parents is non-negotiable, understanding the level and nature of their involvement is essential.

Another purpose of fostering effective communication is to identify the priorities parents have set for their child, as well as their overall parenting priorities. You can gauge a parent's priorities based on the order in which topics are mentioned, the frequency with which they bring up these topics, and the emotion they convey when discussing them.

The topics that parents are most passionate about are the ones in which they show the most emotion when they discuss them. It will be important to keep notes so that you will know what you need to do to capitalize on the positive aspects of your conversation and also what you need to do to offset the challenges you identify during the conversation.

Video: In today's world of technology, video meetings have become very popular. During the COVID-19 pandemic people were stuck in isolation and could not connect in person as much. Many people, including teachers, were not able to go to their workplace and video meetings became the new norm.

Despite all the problems experienced during the pandemic, one benefit for parents and teachers is that it helped people discover this great alternative to meeting in person. Video meetings can be just as effective as in-person meetings. Limitations to this type meeting are the potential for Wi-Fi or equipment issues or cameras not being on or available. Otherwise, this method of communication can be just as effective as an in-person meeting.

Telephone: There will be many times you can't meet in person or by video conference. I would suggest the next best thing to do is to set up a telephone conversation. This will give you an opportunity for dialogue and the ability to find out the same information as though you were in person.

The downside to this type of meeting is that you will not be able to observe nonverbal communication cues, such as body posture or facial expressions. However, this is still better than relying solely on written communication. Written communication is still an option if you cannot meet in person or via telephone.

Text: My preferred form of written communication is text messaging. I place text as the next best after telephone communication. This may or may not be an option. If you are comfortable providing a cell phone number to parents, then you can use this option. If not, then you may consider establishing a Google number as a good texting source.

Many teachers use the school telephone instead of their personal cell phone when communicating with parents. While this is not inherently a negative approach, it does send a message to parents about the boundaries you choose to set. However, if texting is an option, it typically elicits quicker responses from parents since most people tend to respond to text messages promptly. Text messages also allow for the use of emojis, which can help make the conversation feel more personal and meaningful- hopefully, in a positive way. This form of communication may ultimately lead to a phone conversation if the exchange becomes unclear or veers off track for one reason or another. That's perfectly fine, too.

Email: In the event texting is not an option then emailing is the next best option. Email is usually slower than texting, but it is more efficient than sending written notes or letters either by the student or postal service. You must be prepared that a conversation via email can go back and forth for several hours or days. It can also cause people to misinterpret the content being shared.

Regardless of the length or complexity of the email chain, it is best to stay with the conversation until it reaches a conclusion. If at any point there is a concern that the message is being misunderstood, it is crucial to request a switch to one of the more effective communication methods mentioned above. Taking these extra steps will help both teachers and parents feel more comfortable about the conversation.

Notes or Letters: Another available option in the communication process is to send notes or letters using the postal service or the student. While neither of these methods ranks high in efficiency, they can still serve a purpose. I lack confidence that either of these methods will consistently arrive as intended.

The postal service can sometimes misplace letters, and so can students. Students can be slow getting the information to the parent and so can the postal service. Letters can also be intercepted at the mailbox by the student or anyone else. Furthermore, if students think that the information in the letter is going to create a negative outcome for them then the letter they are given to deliver may not arrive to the parent or teacher at all.

Since I don't have much confidence in this method, I feel it should be an additional method of communication as opposed to the only method. You may also use this method after you have already developed an effective communication process with the parent. It can serve a purpose if it is done correctly by all parties involved.

That is the case with all the methods I have described. If you prioritize your methods of communication with your students' parents in this manner, you will stand a better chance of being effective. I must also point out that there might be some extenuating circumstances when none of these methods will work.

If you can't reach a parent using any of the methods I have mentioned, I suggest making a home visit. This should be done in partnership with either a colleague or school administrator. It is best to arrange the visit in advance with parents but since you haven't been able to contact them then this is still an option. Taking this extra step sends a message to parents that you are extremely committed to developing a communication channel with them. This will raise the level of respect parents have for you.

Now that you have a clearer understanding of how to prioritize communication methods, we can move on to the next part of the communication process: being intentional about the content of your communication. So, let's discuss what information should be communicated to your students' parents.

What to Communicate

The content of your communication is of paramount importance. You need to be very clear with parents about what you expect to learn from them and what you need them to know about you. Below are some topics I feel are appropriate to communicate with parents. For each item, I have provided a brief explanation to clarify my rationale.

- **Find out how parents want to be contacted.** You should ask the parents to share the way they prefer to be contacted. For example, you might ask them if they prefer to receive a phone call as opposed to an email. If the parent rarely checks email, then that would not be the best option. Once the contact method is established it is important to consistently use that method when communicating with parents. You should monitor all your communication avenues to make sure you can respond in a timely manner. If parents contact you and there is not a timely response or no response at all, they may eventually stop trying. Therefore, responding timely sends a message to parents that you are being an accommodating partner.

- **Find out when parents prefer to be contacted.** This involves understanding the times of day or days of the week when parents can be reached for non-emergency matters. Some parents may be unable to take calls at work, so it is important to find out which hours are off-limits. Similarly, parents might have specific days off when they are more accessible. Additionally, you should ask parents if there are particular types of behavioral situations-whether positive or negative-involving their child that they wish to be informed about. Naturally, parents should also understand that any such contact restrictions do not apply in the case of an emergency involving their child.

- **Find out details parents can share about their child's personality.** It is important to ask parents to give you details about their child's personality. You should try to find out information such as if they view their child as generally with a positive or negative attitude, easily irritated or calm, aggressive or passive, or energetic or lethargic, to name a few. There may be a few more personality traits parents want to point out, but these are some to help with the conversation. It is important for teachers to know how parents assess their child's personality outside of the school environment because they may or may not see the same version of their child at home that you see at school. This is good information for both teachers and parents to know.

- **Find out which values parents prioritize.** You should ask parents if there are specific values they emphasize at home so that you can help reinforce them in the school setting. When students encounter consistent teachings at home and school, these values are more likely to become ingrained in their daily lives. While it may be challenging to manage all the values collected from parents due to the number of students in your class, this information is particularly useful when engaging with students individually. It also can be information that you can use as extra motivation as you reference the parent communication with the students. Ultimately, if you are aware of the parents' value system, then it can certainly help both you and the parents.

- **Ask parents to share any major events in the student's life.** This should include past, present, or future events. Examples of major events might include the death of a close relative or friend, the birth of a sibling, a neighborhood relocation, or a milestone birthday. Understanding this information is critical because students may exhibit behavior that deviates from their usual character when experiencing events that bring either profound joy or deep sadness. Additionally, ask parents to share information about any notable extracurricular activities, such as a championship game with a club team or an upcoming significant trip or vacation. Being aware of these details enables you to offer the necessary support your students may need to cope with potential disruptions stemming from events outside of school.

- **Ask parents to share their child's interests and preferred activities.** This is good information for you to know. If a parent shares that their child plays a sport or participates in clubs outside of school, you can use this as a conversation topic to build a better relationship with the student. Showing genuine interest in a student's life beyond the classroom communicates that you care about them as individuals, not just as students. This seemingly simple gesture often fosters a deeper level of respect from students toward their teacher. In turn, this respect can inspire students to put forth greater academic effort, potentially leading to improved achievement. On the other side of the conversation, there are some things you need to share with parents about you. This is not an all-inclusive list but it is a good starting place to help parents gain valuable insight into how you operate as their child's teacher. Below are some topics I feel are important to mention when communicating with your students' parents and the rationale for each:

- **Share your philosophy on education.** When you share this with parents, it will help them get a clear understanding of what you believe is the purpose of education. You need to share the importance you place on education for yourself as well as their child. As a teacher, if you don't take the position that educating your students is the top priority, parents have a legitimate right to ask you more probing questions. There are some teachers who believe their main job is to develop students into a person who can work well with others. Although that is important, it should not be the top priority for teachers. Parents should be the primary leader in that area. You must take the position that improving students' academic capabilities and outcomes is your top priority. Whether you want to or not, you will always have to deal with the nonacademic stuff. But, if you allow those things to become a top priority, then students will suffer academically.

- **Share your classroom routines and procedures.** Parents should be informed about the systems you have in place for classroom operations. These might include routines for speaking in class, submitting assignments, student interactions, seating arrangements, and other procedural elements. Teachers who establish clear routines reduce the need for students to constantly have to make decisions on routine matters, thus leading to students being more comfortable in the classroom. The more comfortable students are, the better they can perform academically. When parents know this information, they can help you by reinforcing it at home and it fosters an environment where academics remain the central focus.

- **Share how you manage student behavior.** You should always share with parents how you typically handle inappropriate behavior in the classroom. You should also share how you reward or promote appropriate behavior. Be sure to ask parents how they want to be informed and at what stage in the behavior management process they want to be notified. You should share the consequences you have developed for inappropriate behavior and what behaviors you consider major versus those that are minor. This sends a message to parents regarding where you stand on your priorities and values. By the same token, you should let parents know you are equally consistent in promoting positive behaviors as you are correcting negative behaviors. In either case, you want to determine the point in which you need parents to get involved to either help correct or reinforce the behaviors you have seen in your classroom. The stronger the communication is in this area, the greater the likelihood of student academic success.

- **Share your homework policy**. Clearly outline your stance on homework to parents. Homework can serve different purposes, such as reinforcing concepts already covered, introducing new material requiring independent research, or providing optional practice. Whether homework is optional, mandatory, or graded for accountability, parents should understand your expectations. Whichever policy you set up for homework, it is important to clearly communicate it to parents. It is also important to make parents aware of the resources available to them to support their child when they are attempting to complete the homework assignment. There are many variations of homework policies. My point in this section is not to advocate for a specific homework policy. I have already stated my position on homework in Chapter 5. The point here is to make you aware that parents need to be informed of all the details of your policy so they can best support both you and their child.

- **Share your make-up policy for assignments.** Inform parents about your stance on accepting late assignments. Some teachers allow all assignments to be submitted after the deadline, some permit certain assignments to be turned in late with or without penalties, while others handle late submissions on a case-by-case basis. Still others may allow late assignment submissions without penalty up to the end of a grading period. There are too many make-up policy variations to name them all in this section. You certainly need to make parents aware of your assignment make-up policy because many times it can be more about the student's level of responsibility than the actual assignment itself. This can help parents avoid allowing a nonacademic factor to determine their child's academic outcome.

- **Share your policy for retakes on tests and quizzes.** This is similar to the previous topic on assignments but could be much more critical since tests and quizzes often constitute a higher percentage of a student's final grade. Some teachers allow one or more retake opportunities, while some may not allow any at all. If there are no retakes allowed, it places greater pressure on students to be more prepared prior to the test or quiz. This might increase the burden on parents to help their child develop a study plan. On the other hand, if you allow retakes, even if it is only one, it could open the door to students possibly not taking their initial preparation seriously. I suggest that regardless of whether you do or don't allow retakes, it is important to share with parents the necessity of having their child prepare as if it would be their only opportunity. This will get students in the habit of trying their best regardless of what your policy permits.

- **Share your teaching style.** Teachers should let parents know how they implement their lesson plans. It is good to share the approximate time you usually spend on activities such as lecturing or teacher demonstrations (teacher-focused), versus activities involving interactive student group work or hands-on opportunities (student-focused). This can help parents determine how to support their child along the way. If parents know their child is a "sit-and-get" type of learner, then teacher-centered lessons may work just fine. However, if their child needs to be interactive in the learning process, parents will know they might have to follow up with you to see if you can provide additional resources to supplement the learning process when lessons are primarily teacher-centered. The more aligned the teaching styles are with the students' natural learning preferences, the easier the parents' job will be. However, you should stress to parents the need to help their child adapt to various teaching styles because you cannot always teach exclusively to a particular learning style. Also, let parents know that as their child is exposed to and adapts to a variety of teaching styles, it will eventually help them improve academically.

- **Share the ways you participate in school clubs or other nonacademic programs.** This is additional information that can help parents understand the extent to which you are invested in the overall school community. Generally, teachers who are involved in other school activities tend to be more student-centered in their approach. These teachers usually are the ones who develop more meaningful relationships with students. I am certainly not saying that teachers who aren't involved in non-academic programs don't develop strong relationships with their students or aren't student-centered. What I am saying is that it is much more likely for good relationships to be established when teachers are also involved in non-academic programs by serving in roles such as club sponsors or coaches. When teachers build strong relationships with their students, there is a greater chance that students will achieve at higher academic levels. Therefore, I suggest that all teachers consider participating in some type of extracurricular activities involving students, either as a coach, club sponsor, or spectator. Both students and parents will notice! These are some areas I feel are important for teachers to discuss when communicating with parents. You might have other areas you feel are important to add, but I believe these are essential as a starting point. Regardless of the specific areas you cover during your communication, it is most important that you don't miss the opportunity to have a conversation with parents. The students' academic success is too important to skip this step in building an effective partnership with parents. Along with the importance of communicating with parents, it is helpful to make parents aware of your desire to have them become an active participant in their child's education process. In the next section, I will share some details on how to encourage effective parent participation in the school-home-community partnership.

Parent Participation

Parent participation is an important part of students' success. Students need the support of their parents as they navigate through school. Throughout your career, you will encounter many parents who may or may not be visibly involved in their child's school experience. Regardless of whether the parents are visibly present at the school building, I have found that most parents do participate in their child's education in some form. I believe this is an important assumption all teachers should embrace in order to have the right mindset when communicating with parents.

Based on this line of thinking, it is up to you as the students' teacher to help parents find ways to become actively involved. The level of their participation will depend on their unique circumstances. Some parents have unlimited time to devote to their child's education while others can barely carve out a few minutes. Therefore, you should offer parents both in-school and out-of-school opportunities to support their child.

In the next sections, I will share two sets of bulleted suggestions. The first list includes ways parents can participate in activities that generally take place at or around the school building. These items can be viewed as visible support. The second list includes ways parents can participate in activities that take place primarily at home or away from the school building. These items are generally not seen by school personnel but can be very impactful, nonetheless.

Participation at School

The items below are ways parents can provide visible support at or around the school building. Some of the items might be necessary during the school day, while others might take place outside of normal school hours. When parents engage in these activities, it positively impacts the school-home-community partnership. Here are some school-related activities you can suggest to parents:

- **Join the school's parent-teacher organization.** This is an important step for parents to show they want to officially become an active partner with their child's school. Parent-teacher groups are known by different names, such as Parent Teacher Student Association (PTSA), Parent Teacher Association (PTA), Parent Teacher Organization (PTO), and so on. Regardless of the official name of the school's parent-teacher group, you should encourage parents to join and become an active participant. Parent-teacher groups are typically operated by parents with the primary goal of supporting the teachers, administrators, and students. The support offered depends largely on the commitment of the members. A well-functioning group will have active representation that includes teachers, students, parents, building administration, and community business partners.

- **Attend as many school events as possible.** Attending school events is another way for parents to demonstrate that they are engaged and invested as a parent. Not only should parents attend their own child's events, but they should be encouraged to attend additional events as well. I suggest this for two reasons. One reason is that it gives parents a broader understanding of other programs the school offers, enabling them to determine more objectively whether they would like to encourage their child to participate. The second reason is that it shows parents' overall investment in the school community, regardless of whether their child is directly involved. Undoubtedly, you have had positive conversations with other teachers and administrators about parents who exemplify this level of commitment.

- **Look for volunteer opportunities.** Most often, schools don't have all the personnel they need to ensure everything gets done. There are times when an extra pair of hands can make a significant difference. It is good to think of as many ways as possible for parents to assist. For example, you may need help displaying student projects around the school. Parents might be able to provide such assistance if it's arranged after the school day. You will probably get more volunteers for requests that provide parents with opportunities that align with their schedules and do not interfere with work commitments. There are always volunteer opportunities at sporting events, festivals, or school dances.

- **Look for opportunities to make donations.** Schools sponsor many programs and events throughout the school year. In my experience, teachers usually need more materials than the budget allows. This opens the door for making requests to parents to help fill the school budget deficits during the school year. Don't be afraid to ask parents for donations to help with events, programs, or lesson activities. You may also ask parents to donate in other forms, such as stocking a food pantry or clothes closet, providing school supplies for you and your students, offering gift cards or prizes for incentives, or donating snacks for school athletic teams or clubs. These are just a few examples of ways parents can donate. I am sure you will encounter shortfalls during the school year that will create opportunities to send out requests to parents for donations. I suggest you use parents as a resource but be careful not to abuse it.

- **Make connections with school support personnel.** Encourage parents to get to know the school secretaries, cafeteria manager, school nurse, and guidance counselors. Although these people support students primarily outside of the classroom, they are important people that parents should know. The secretaries are the gatekeepers who can help parents get what they need, or they can intentionally or unintentionally create some significant roadblocks. The cafeteria manager and other lunchroom staff can provide parents with the details on the school's nutrition program. Parents should communicate to them any special dietary needs or limits they may want to place on their child's lunch account. The school nurse can help parents understand what the school's rules are for both prescription and nonprescription medicines. Guidance counselors can provide parents with insight into their child's social and emotional wellbeing. They can also help parents locate both academic support and career exploration resources. Hopefully, you can share the items on this bulleted list so that parents are more aware of how they can become active and visible supporters at their child's school. However, there are also ways parents can actively participate without requiring the visibility of showing up in the school building or attending events and activities. In the next section, I will share some ways parents can become active participants in the school-home-community partnership outside of the school building.

Participation at Home

The list of items in this section outlines some ways parents can actively participate at home or away from school grounds. These items should provide support for their child while also helping to supplement what you are doing at school. Here are some things you might suggest to parents.

- **Create a designated place for homework.** A dedicated workspace should be provided for students to use for studying, doing homework, or completing projects. Many students think they can watch TV or socialize while trying to complete homework or study. They believe they can concentrate amidst noise and distractions, but such environments hinder their ability to retain information effectively. There are some exceptions, but I would encourage parents not to take that chance. Therefore, you should suggest to parents that they find a quiet space to designate as a study area for their child. If space is limited, parents may need to pause other household activities at a specific time and location to create a conducive learning atmosphere. Doing so emphasizes to their child that the time spent in that space is focused on achieving academic success.

- **Create a system to organize school obligations.** Encourage parents to develop a way to help their child stay organized to avoid overlooking assignment deadlines, test dates, and project deadlines. A good strategy might be to include incremental goals to complete steps leading up to final submissions or test dates. For example, parents may want to have their child document milestone dates, such as when a certain portion of a school project will be completed or when supplies need to be purchased for the project. This approach can help minimize stress for their child. Achieving consistent progress also fosters a sense of accomplishment and boosts morale. In addition, parents may want to include school events and activities in their organizational system for a comprehensive view of all commitments. This system will support their child and the school, even though it is managed primarily outside of the school.

- **Reinforce school priorities at home.** When you shared your priorities during the conversations you have had with parents, you should ask them to help by reinforcing some of those priorities at home. This should assist you with classroom management and organization while also giving the student the foundation you expect them to have. There will also be times during the year when certain trends are popular with students. A couple of notable times might be Halloween or St. Patrick's Day. Students tend to get caught up in candy trading during Halloween or pinching each other on St. Patrick's Day. It is during these times that you may need to send home reminders to parents to help their children make good choices. That is where their reinforcement at home might make a tremendous difference on whether their child remains focused or lets the distractions negatively impact their educational outcomes.

- **Have regular conversations about school.** Make parents aware of the importance of routinely asking their child questions about the school day. Some parents may not know how to have those conversations, so don't hesitate to provide specific conversation prompts they can use with their child. You might suggest asking their child to share something they learned in a few classes, particularly those posing challenges. Parents can also inquire about their child's social interactions at school. This information can help parents gain insights into their child's social network and, if necessary, follow up with you regarding any concerns. While you cannot discuss other students with parents, you can share any general concerns about their child's associations. You might also suggest to parents to make time to probe into their child's overall feelings about school. If there's any dissatisfaction, parents can delve deeper to help address the issue and reshape their child's perspective. Overall, these conversations should help parents maintain an accurate understanding of their child's school experience. Academic success is much more likely when parents consistently communicate with their child about what's happening at school.

- **Use resources to support the academic needs and career interests.** The primary goal of schools is to prepare students for the next level. Elementary school teachers must equip their students for middle school. Middle school educators must prepare students for the challenges of high school, while high school teachers aim to ensure students are ready for higher education or the workforce. Thus, providing parents with resources to supplement what is being taught at school is crucial. Encourage parents to conduct additional research to identify effective academic tools that can support their child's learning journey. Parents should also be urged to explore opportunities that might inspire career exploration for their children, such as summer camps, weekend workshops, or job-shadowing programs. Career interests can be powerful motivators for students. While these interests often develop in elementary school, they may evolve as students are exposed to various careers. You should encourage parents to engage with their child on this topic during the upper elementary years, though this engagement may occur earlier or later depending on the child's readiness. However, parents should be encouraged to begin this process no later than freshman year of high school. By this point, parents should assist their child in gaining a clear understanding of the prerequisites for the desired career path and the requirements of the college or trade school they plan to pursue. Consider directing parents to your school's guidance counselor, who can provide valuable information and support to aid their child's academic and career journey. The items shared thus far reflect key areas of focus when striving to develop an effective school-home-community partnership as it relates to parents. However, this is by no means an exhaustive list. As with all the other topics covered, adjustments must be made to accommodate the uniqueness of each child. No single solution will be effective for all children. Regardless of the specific adjustments made, the main goal is to develop active engagement and positive participation in the school-home-community partnership. It is important to communicate with parents the importance of sending a message to their child that there is a strong partnership between their teachers and their parents. The other aspect of the school-home-community partnership is the community. It is important for teachers to establish strong community support from various groups and organizations. In the next section I will share some helpful community resources that can be valuable for both students, parents, and teachers.

Community Groups

Community groups can serve as invaluable partners for both educators and families. These groups offer activities and resources designed to enhance the well-being of children and enrich their lives. As the third pillar of the school-home-community partnership, these organizations provide a diverse range of programs and support.

To determine which groups to include in this partnership, it is essential to conduct thorough research to gather information about each organization under consideration. This step is critical because, while many groups contribute positively to their communities, some may involve individuals or circumstances that are not appropriate for students or families.

The community groups listed below are some that I have found to be appropriate. Most of them I have firsthand knowledge of how they operate. The ones I have not used, I have examined them at the local community level in my role as educator and school administrator. However, you should not rely solely on my judgment. It is up to you to screen the community groups in your local area to determine if they are a good fit. Some examples of community groups to include might be:

- Big Brothers Big Sisters of America

- Boy/Girl Scouts

- Boys & Girls Club of America

- 4-H

- YMCA/YWCA

- Community Youth Programs

- Recreational Sports Leagues

- Junior Achievement

- PTA/PTSA/PTO

- Civic Organizations

Based on your needs and the needs of your students, each of these groups can be useful. Big Brothers Big Sisters of America provides one-on-one mentoring. Boy/Girl Scouts provides life skills, character building, and mentorship. Boys & Girls Club, 4-H, YMCA, and YWCA provide a wide range of programs and activities for youth. Community Youth Programs and Recreational Sports Leagues, typically managed by local county or city recreation departments, provide free and low-cost activities and athletics for youth in the community.

Junior Achievement provides training on business ownership and financial literacy for youth. PTA/PTSA/PTO, as I mentioned earlier, are parent-led groups in schools that provide support for teachers and students. Civic Organizations such as Kiwanis or Rotary Clubs offer a range of programs and funding for schools.

All these community groups can provide meaningful support. Please note that this is not an all-inclusive list by any means nor is it a guarantee that these groups will be a good fit for you or your students and parents.

Each group you consider will need to be screened so that you are comfortable using them and recommending them to parents. To help you in the screening process, you might consider getting answers to the following questions:

- What events does this group sponsor?

- What events has it sponsored in the past?

- What are the ongoing or seasonal activities?

- Who funds the group (government, private donors, etc.)?

- What is the group's mission? What is its primary purpose?

- What is its vision? What is the ultimate goal the group wants to achieve?

- How does the group operate?

- Who does the group primarily serve?

- Is the group teacher/student/parent friendly? How are clients or customers treated?

- How do the workers and volunteers act? Are they good role models?

The answers to these questions can help you determine whether a group aligns with your goals and those of your students and parents. It is worth noting that each group functions differently within its local community. Just as no two individuals are identical, no two branches of a community group operate in the exact same way.

In this chapter, I have aimed to provide insights into establishing a meaningful and effective school-home-community partnership. While many of the topics covered here could be explored in greater depth, my goal has been to offer a concise yet comprehensive foundation for building strong partnerships. As I have emphasized in earlier chapters, the success of these strategies ultimately depends on their thoughtful and intentional implementation by educators.

Developing a thriving school-home-community partnership is your responsibility, and its success lies in your hands.

Final Thoughts

Throughout this book, I have shared quite a few strategies designed to help you collaborate effectively with students, parents, colleagues, community groups, and others to enhance the likelihood of achieving success for both you and your students.

As a teacher in today's challenging educational landscape, you may sometimes feel overwhelmed by the myriad of issues you are facing. Educating students is no small task; in fact, being an educator is arguably the most difficult profession in our society. You only have a finite opportunity with each student, and you cannot afford to take chances, hoping for the best outcome. You must be purposeful and deliberate in your approach.

I hope this book has provided you with reassurance by offering practical strategies that empower you to become the best teacher you can be. As I have emphasized throughout, not all strategies and suggestions will work for every teacher, student, or parent. Experiment with them, identify what resonates with your unique circumstances, and adapt those strategies to fit your needs. However, it is crucial to avoid abandoning a strategy too hastily.

The success of any strategy depends significantly on the degree of consistency with which it is implemented. I believe that these strategies, when applied consistently, will make you a more effective teacher. In turn, this will ensure that your students reap meaningful benefits. I am confident that these strategies are truly *"Teaching Strategies of Success!"*

For additional support on ways to consistently implement the strategies in this book, you may visit Solomon and Associates Consulting Group website at www.cbsolomongroup.com to submit a request or call us at (770)800-1685. We are available to provide professional development and resources to teachers, administrators, parents, and school districts.

ADDITIONAL RESOURCES

The resources on this list are not meant to be an endorsement of their effectiveness. The items provided are only to help with further exploration of the topics listed in the chapters of the book. It is up to the reader to validate the credibility of any of the resources on this list. Except for the author's own published material, there is not a direct or indirect financial benefit from any resource on this list.

Chapter 1

Instructional Practices Inventory (IPI) Website – Dr. Jerry Valentine
https://www.ipistudentengagement.com/

Chapter 2

7 Ways to build a positive student teacher relationship
https://nearpod.com/blog/student-teacher-relationships/

Teacher Student Relationships Matter
https://www.gse.harvard.edu/ideas/usable-knowledge/21/03/teacher-student-relationships-matter

The Importance of Student-Teacher Relationships
https://ecampusontario.pressbooks.pub/educ5202/chapter/the-importance-of-student-teacher-relationships/

Improving Students' Relationships with Teachers to Provide Essential Supports for Learning
https://www.apa.org/education-career/k12/relationships

Chapter 3

Brookfield, S. D.(2017). Becoming a critically reflective teacher. Reflective Practices in Education: A Primer for Practitioners
https://www.lifescied.org/doi/10.1187/cbe.22-07-0148

Qualities of a Good Teacher: The 14 Qualities That Top Our List
https://www.nu.edu/blog/qualities-of-a-good-teacher/

The Most Important Qualities That Make a Good Teacher
https://www.teachersoftomorrow.org/blog/insights/good-teacher-qualities/

What Works – and What Doesn't – in Teacher PD
https://www.edweek.org/leadership/what-works-and-what-doesnt-in-teacher-pd/2022/10

Effective Teacher Professional Development
https://learningpolicyinstitute.org/product/effective-teacher-professional-development-report

Chapter 4

Wong, H. K. & Wong, R. T. (2018). The First Days of School: How to Be an Effective Teacher, 5th Ed.

Clark, R. (2019). The Essential 55: An Award-Winning Educator's Rules for Discovering the Successful Student in Every Child, Revised and Updated.

Positive Behavioral Interventions and Supports (PBIS)
https://www.pbis.org/
https://pbisnetwork.org/resources/introduction-to-swpbis/

Setting Classroom Expectations the First Week of School (PBIS)
https://www.pbisrewards.com/blog/setting-classroom-expectations/

6 Steps to Establish Behavior Expectations [+ Downloadable Worksheets]
https://www.panoramaed.com/blog/establishing-and-teaching-behavior-expectations

Five Discipline Strategies That Preserve Dignity
https://www.responsiveclassroom.org/five-discipline-strategies-that-preserve-dignity/

Consequences That Teach Better Behavior (Instead of Punish)
https://heidisongs.blog/consequences-that-teach-better-behavior-instead-of-punish/

Chapter 5

Richard Dufour – What is a Professional Learning Community?
https://allthingsplc.info/wp-content/uploads/2023/10/DuFourWhatIsAProfessionalLearningCommunity.pdf

Professional Learning Communities
https://www.theprincipalsplaybook.com/instructional-leadership/plc-dufour

How Different Assessments and Measures Can Help Inform Student Growth
https://www.erblearn.org/blog/different-types-of-assessments-in-education/

Creating a Homework Policy with Meaning and Purpose
https://www.thoughtco.com/creating-a-homework-policy-with-meaning-and-purpose-3194513

The Dos and Don'ts of Good Homework Policy
https://www.middleweb.com/33142/the-dos-and-donts-of-good-homework-policy/

20 Differentiated Instruction Strategies and Examples(+Downloadable List)
https://www.prodigygame.com/main-en/blog/differentiated-instruction-strategies-examples-download/

15 Teaching Styles: The Complete Guide for Effective Teaching
https://scienceandliteracy.org/teaching-styles/

The 5 Most Effective Teaching Styles (Pros and Cons of Each)
https://www.thinkific.com/blog/teaching-styles/

The 7 Main Types of Learning Styles (And How To Teach To Them)
https://www.thinkific.com/blog/learning-styles/

Differentiated Instruction
https://ctl.stanford.edu/differentiated-instruction

Creating Meaningful Grading Policies
https://www.edutopia.org/article/creating-meaningful-grading-policies/

The Problem with Grading
https://www.gse.harvard.edu/ideas/ed-magazine/23/05/problem-grading

What the F? Grading strategies for early career teachers
https://www.eschoolnews.com/innovative-teaching/2023/03/09/what-the-f-grading-strategies-for-early-career-teachers/

The Case Against Zeros in Grading

https://www.edutopia.org/article/case-against-zeros-grading

How to Use Technology in the Classroom: Benefits and Effects

https://drexel.edu/soe/resources/student-teaching/advice/how-to-use-technology-in-the-classroom/

7 Ways Technology in the Classroom Enhances Student Success

https://explorance.com/blog/7-reasons-students-need-technology-classroom/

When Special and General Educators Collaborate, Everybody Wins

https://ascd.org/el/articles/when-special-and-general-educators-collaborate-everybody-wins

How to Practice Culturally Relevant Pedagogy

https://www.teachforamerica.org/stories/culturally-relevant-pedagogy

Culturally Responsive Teaching

https://www.nationalequityproject.org/culturally-responsive-teaching

Standardized Tests

https://www.britannica.com/procon/standardized-tests-debate

Chapter 6

Supporting Teachers as an Administrator: 5 Helpful Tips for School Leaders

https://strobeleducation.com/blog/supporting-teachers-as-an-administrator/

Mentoring Beginning Teachers (The Alberta Teachers' Association):

https://ncee.org/wp-content/uploads/2017/01/Alb-non-AV-18-ATA-Mentoring-beginning-teachers.pdf

Using Social Media to Build a Personal Learning Network
https://www.edutopia.org/article/using-social-media-build-personal-learning-network/

Chapter 7

Solomon, C. B. (2024). Parenting Strategies of Success.
https://a.co/d/7Tybcff

Center for Family Engagement:
https://www.pta.org/docs/default-source/files/cfe/2023/center-for-family-engagement-resource-list.pdf

15 Advocacy Groups Championing Teachers and Learning Across the U.S.
https://blog.planbook.com/championing-teachers/

Cultivating Highly Successful Parent Teacher Communication
https://www.thoughtco.com/tips-for-highly-successful-parent-teacher-communication-3194676

School Communication Policy
https://www.thoughtco.com/school-communication-policy-3194670

www.ingramcontent.com/pod-product-compliance
Lightning Source LLC
Chambersburg PA
CBHW052022030426
42335CB00026B/3252